ALIEN INVASION: SPORTS EDITION

SLAPSHOT

ICING ANGER

by Josh Anderson & Gil Conrad
illustrated by Turner Lange

Published in the United States of America by Cherry Lake Publishing Group
Ann Arbor, Michigan
www.cherrylakepublishing.com

Reading Adviser: Beth Walker Gambro, MS, Ed., Reading Consultant, Yorkville, IL

Book Design: Book Buddy Media

Photo Credits: page 1: ©DigitalVision Vectors / Getty Images; page 7: ©Hulton Archive / Getty Images; page 13: ©Todd Warshaw / Allsport / Getty Images; page 27: ©Krakenimages.com / Shutterstock; clipboard background: ©t_kimura / Getty Images; galaxy background: ©vi73777 / Getty Images; hockey background: ©Grushin / Shutterstock

Torch Graphic Press is an imprint of Cherry Lake Publishing Group.

Library of Congress Cataloging-in-Publication Data has been filed and is available at catalog.loc.gov

Cherry Lake Publishing Group would like to acknowledge the work of the Partnership for 21st Century Learning, a Network of Battelle for Kids. Please visit http://www.battelleforkids.org/networks/p21 for more information.

Printed in the United States of America
Corporate Graphics

TABLE OF CONTENTS

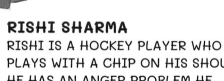

RISHI SHARMA
RISHI IS A HOCKEY PLAYER WHO
PLAYS WITH A CHIP ON HIS SHOULDER.
HE HAS AN ANGER PROBLEM HE
NEEDS TO GET UNDER CONTROL.

MIKKI
MIKKI IS AN ALIEN FROM
PLANET KOPITER. HIS SPORT
IS GRILLETTE. HE HAS
WORKED HARD TO KEEP HIS
COOL UNDER PRESSURE.

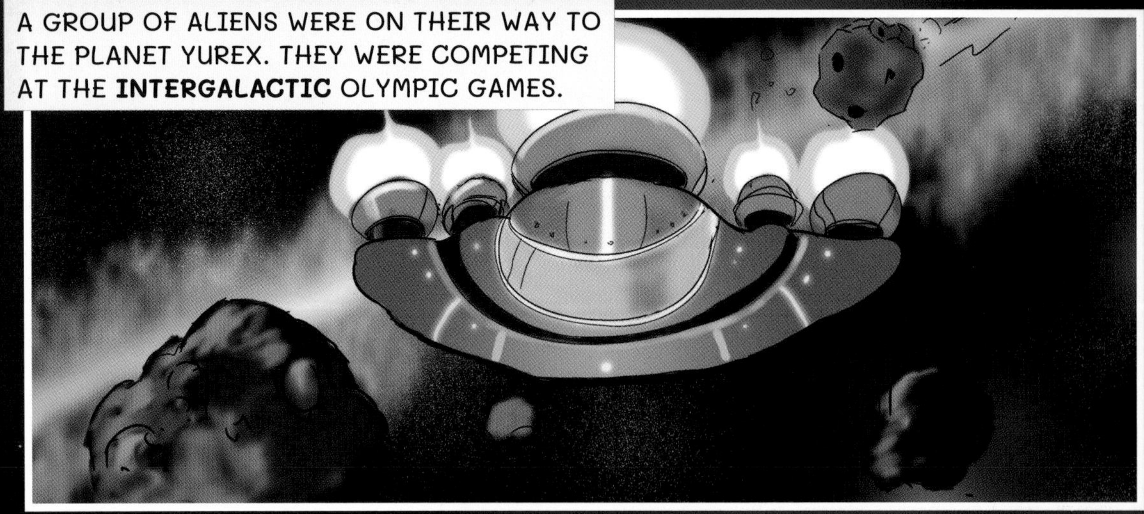
A GROUP OF ALIENS WERE ON THEIR WAY TO THE PLANET YUREX. THEY WERE COMPETING AT THE **INTERGALACTIC** OLYMPIC GAMES.

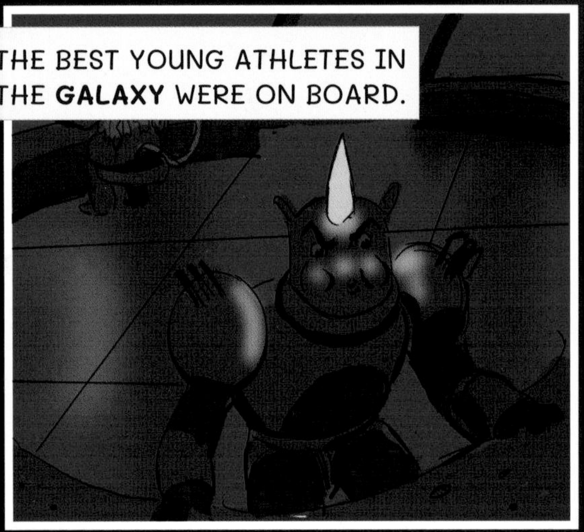
THE BEST YOUNG ATHLETES IN THE **GALAXY** WERE ON BOARD.

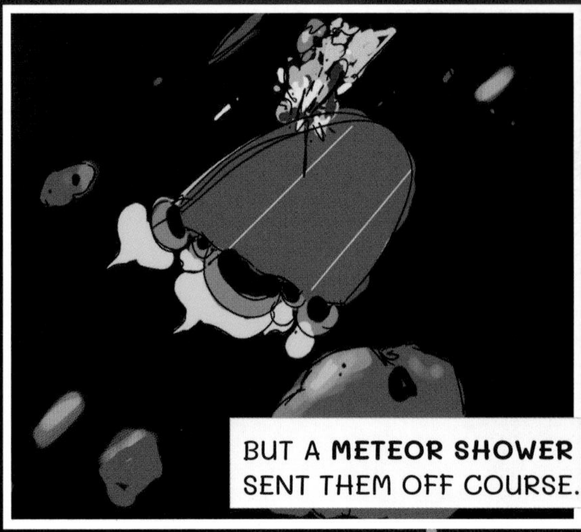
BUT A **METEOR SHOWER** SENT THEM OFF COURSE.

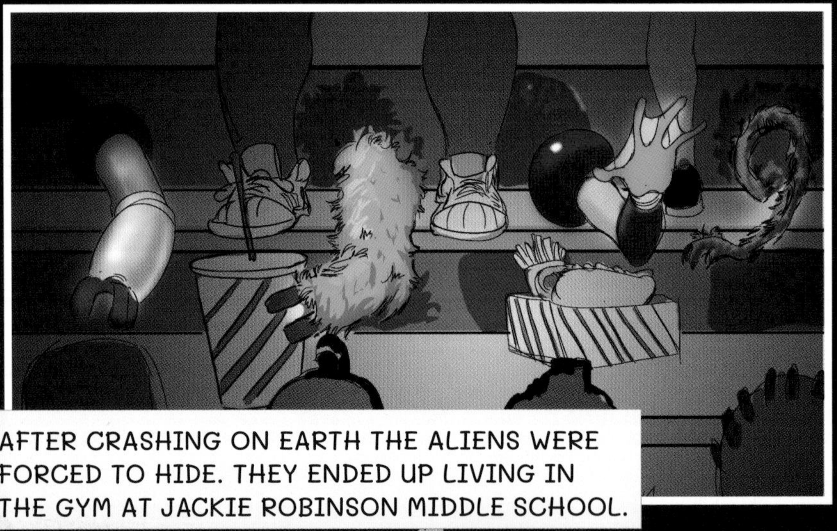
AFTER CRASHING ON EARTH THE ALIENS WERE FORCED TO HIDE. THEY ENDED UP LIVING IN THE GYM AT JACKIE ROBINSON MIDDLE SCHOOL.

intergalactic: between galaxies in space

galaxy: a system of stars and their solar systems

meteor shower: a group of space rocks that fall as they enter Earth's atmosphere

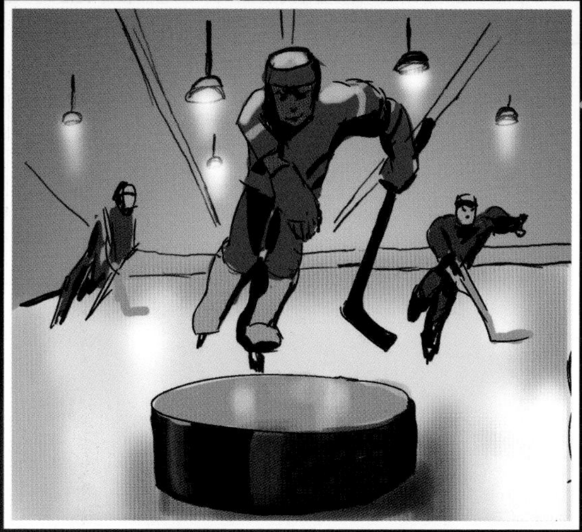

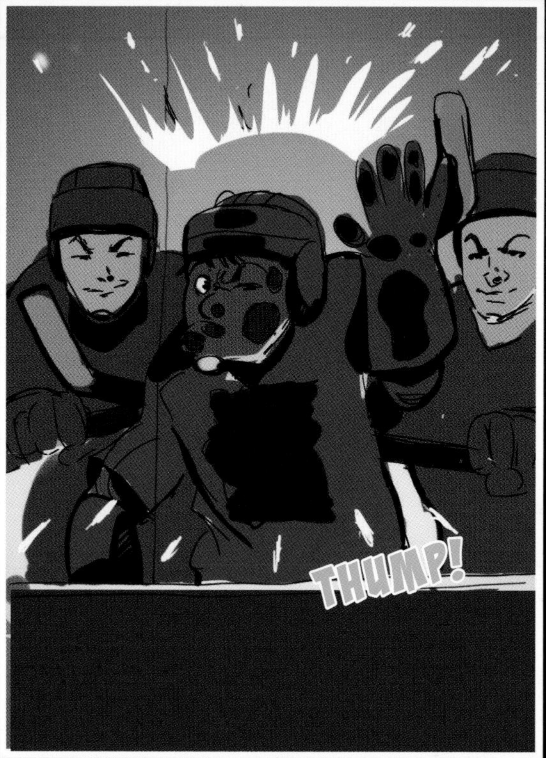
THUMP!

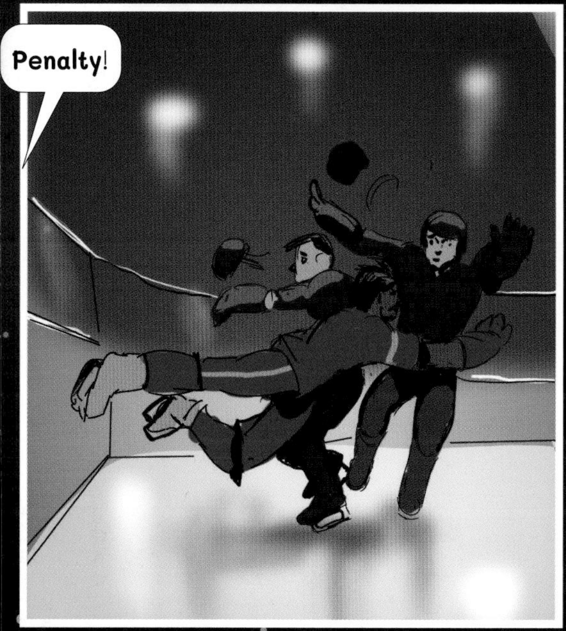
Penalty!

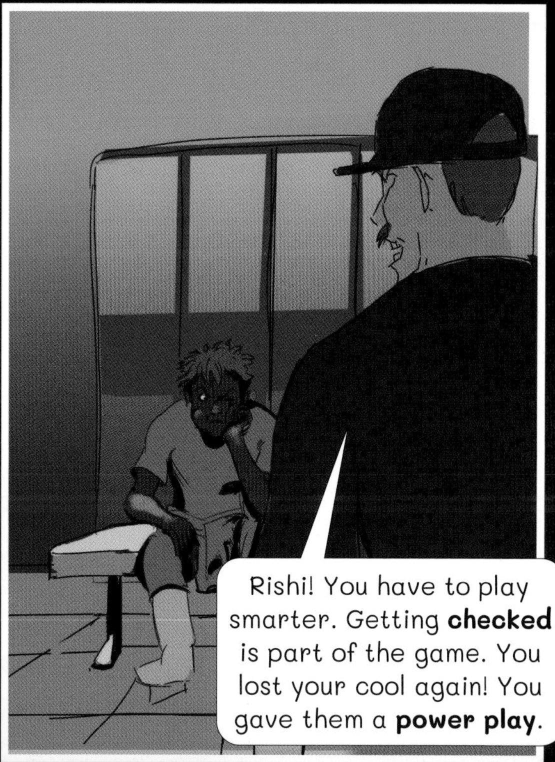
Rishi! You have to play smarter. Getting **checked** is part of the game. You lost your cool again! You gave them a **power play**.

penalty: a punishment for breaking the rules

checked: when one player crashes into the player controlling the puck

power play: a period of time during a hockey game where at least one opposing player is in the penalty box

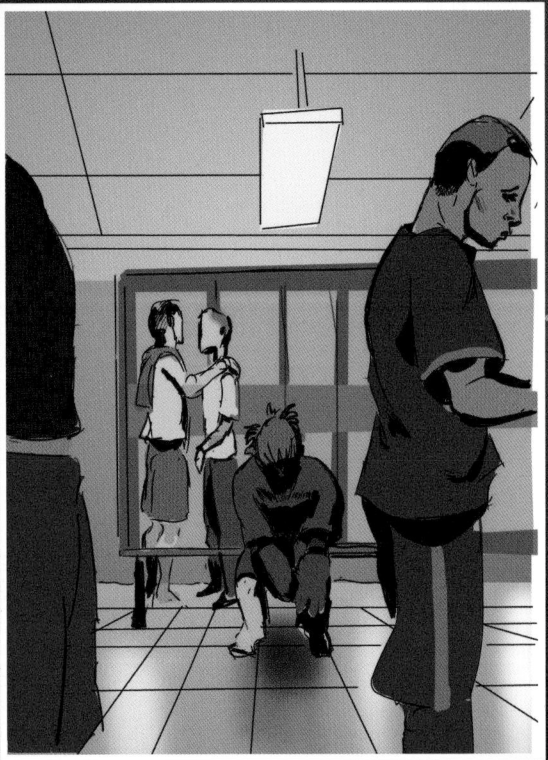

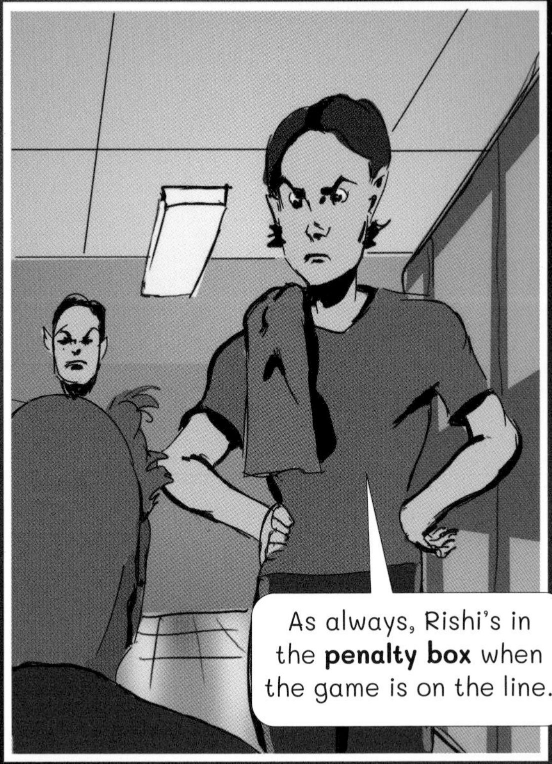
As always, Rishi's in the **penalty box** when the game is on the line.

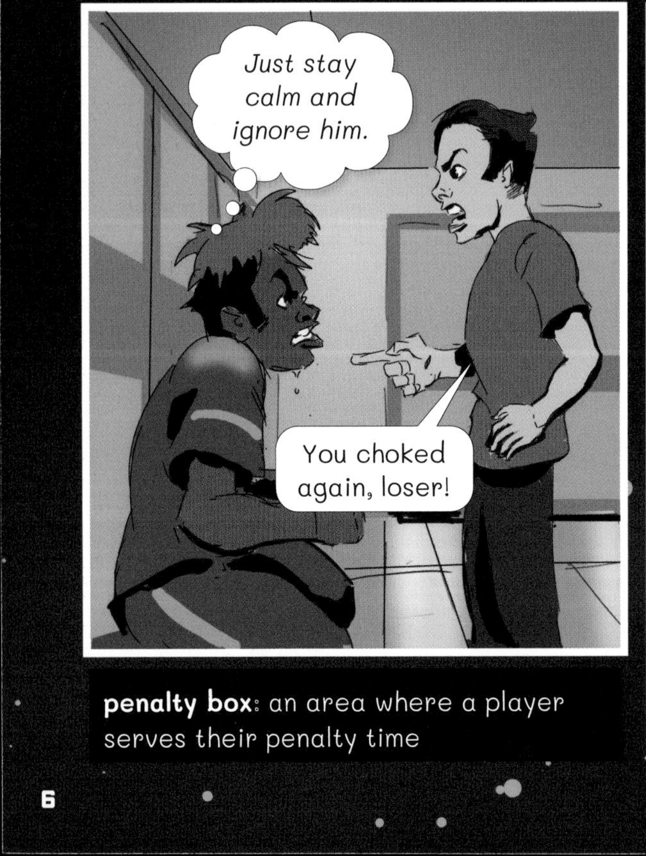
Just stay calm and ignore him.
You choked again, loser!

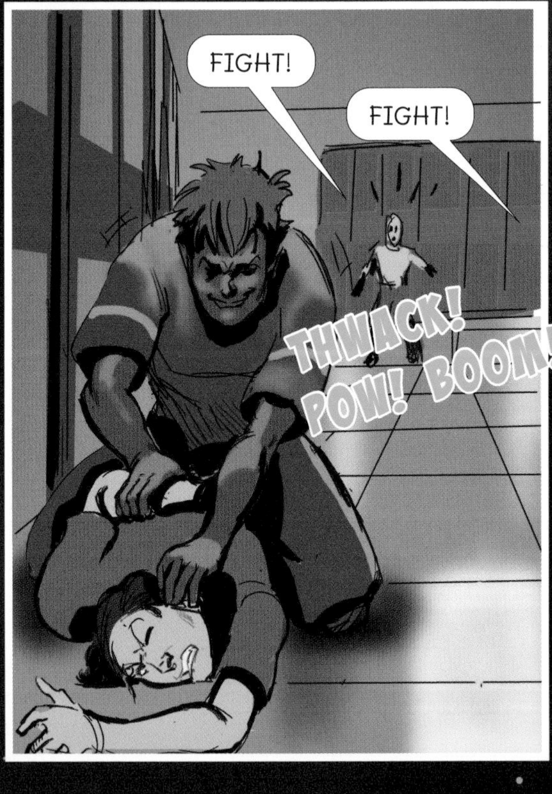
FIGHT!
FIGHT!
THWACK! POW! BOOM!

penalty box: an area where a player serves their penalty time

HISTORY OF HOCKEY

Ice hockey is a game of speed! Skates help players travel quickly. The first game was likely played in Canada in the mid-1800s. The first indoor game was played in 1875.

The National Hockey League (NHL) was founded in 1917. Today, there are 31 teams located in Canada and the United States. The teams compete for the Stanley Cup every year.

More than a million people play hockey in North America. The rules have remained almost the same since the league began. Each team has 6 players. Five players use a stick to pass and shoot the puck. They score by shooting the puck into the net guarded by the sixth player, the goalie.

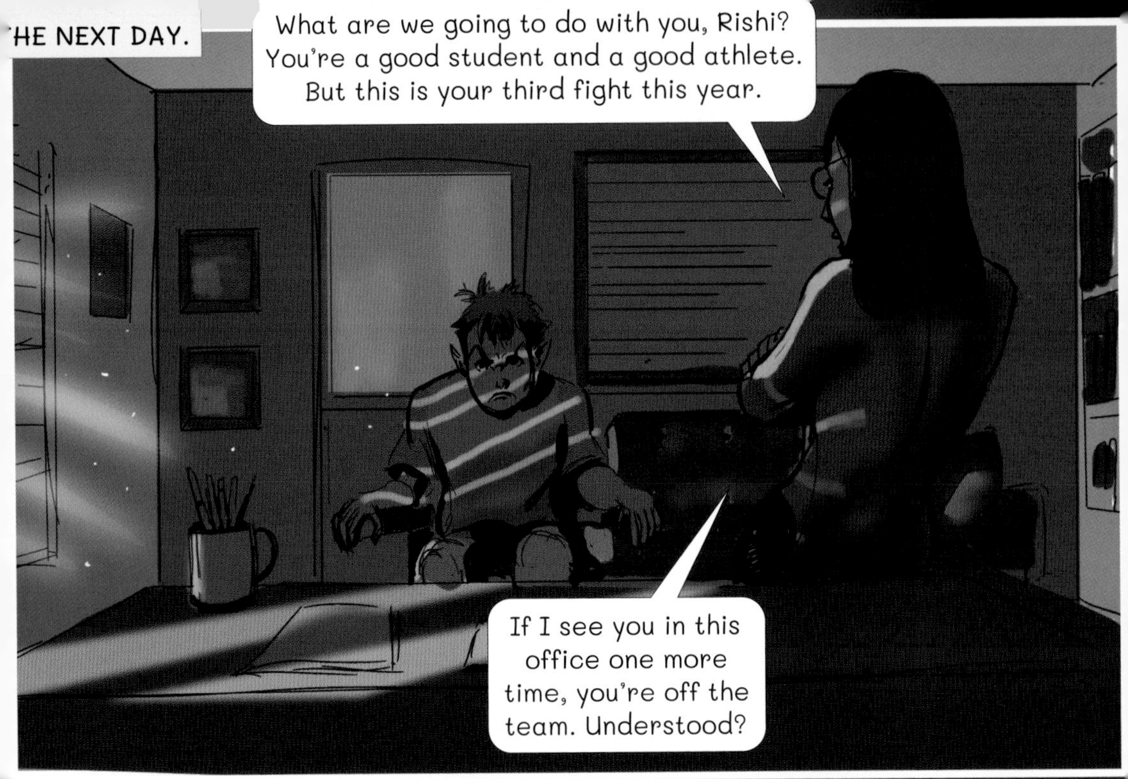
THE NEXT DAY.
What are we going to do with you, Rishi? You're a good student and a good athlete. But this is your third fight this year.
If I see you in this office one more time, you're off the team. Understood?

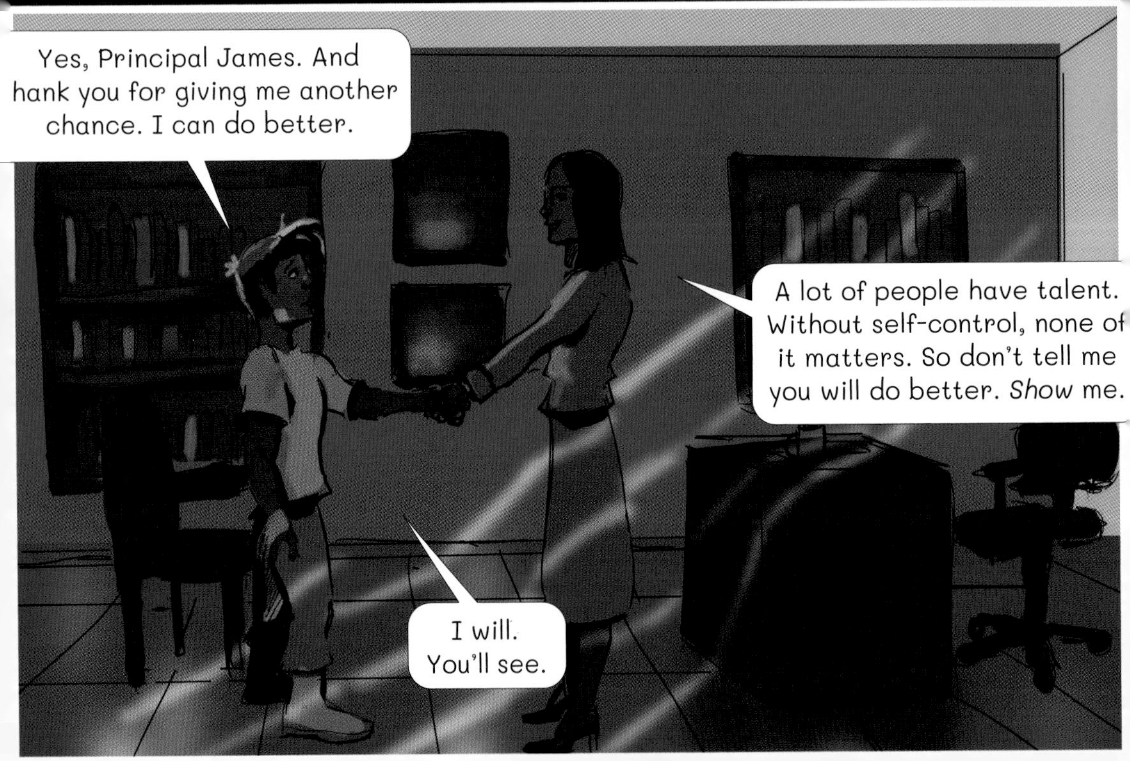
Yes, Principal James. And hank you for giving me another chance. I can do better.
A lot of people have talent. Without self-control, none of it matters. So don't tell me you will do better. *Show* me.
I will. You'll see.

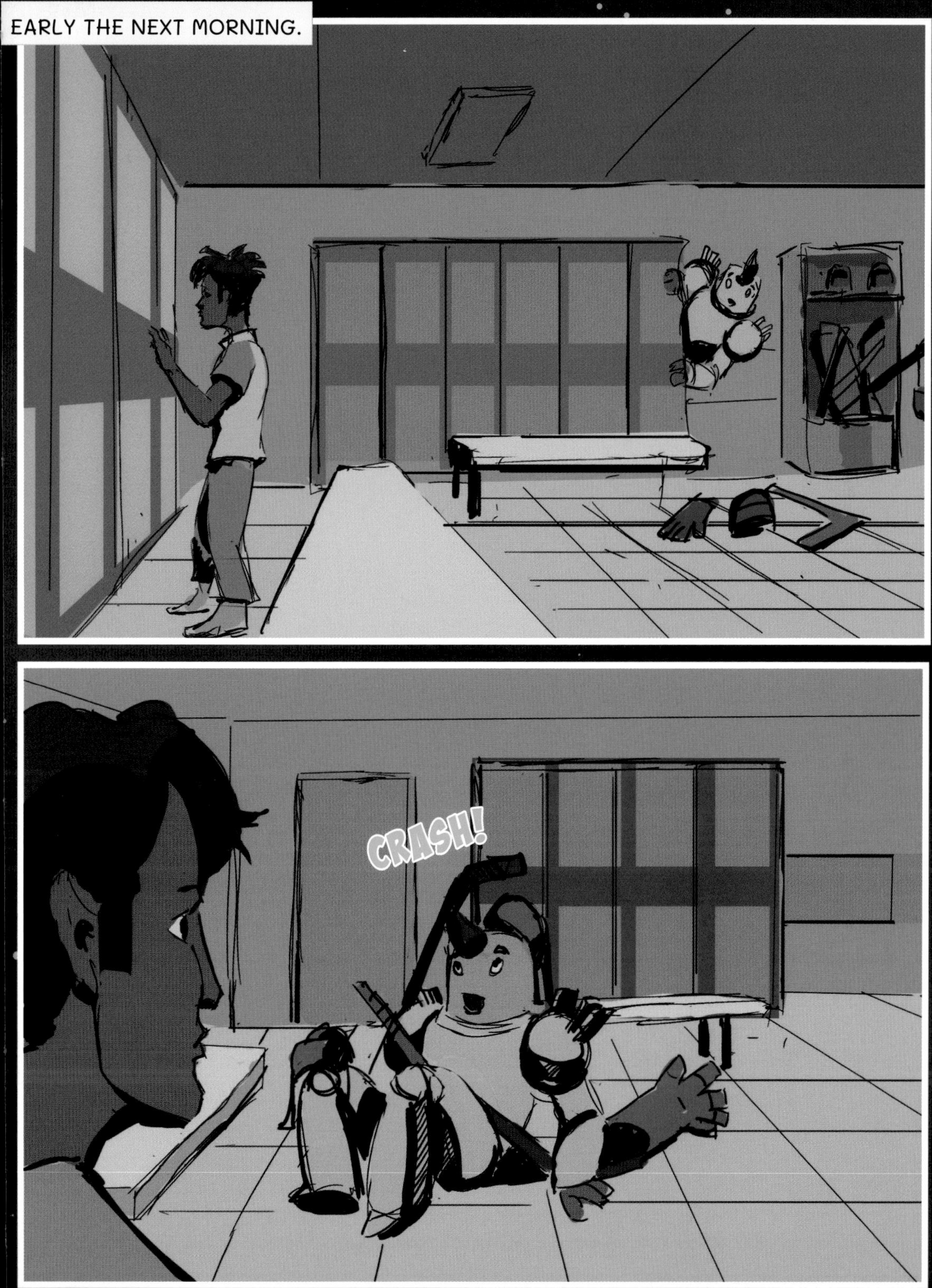
EARLY THE NEXT MORNING.
CRASH!

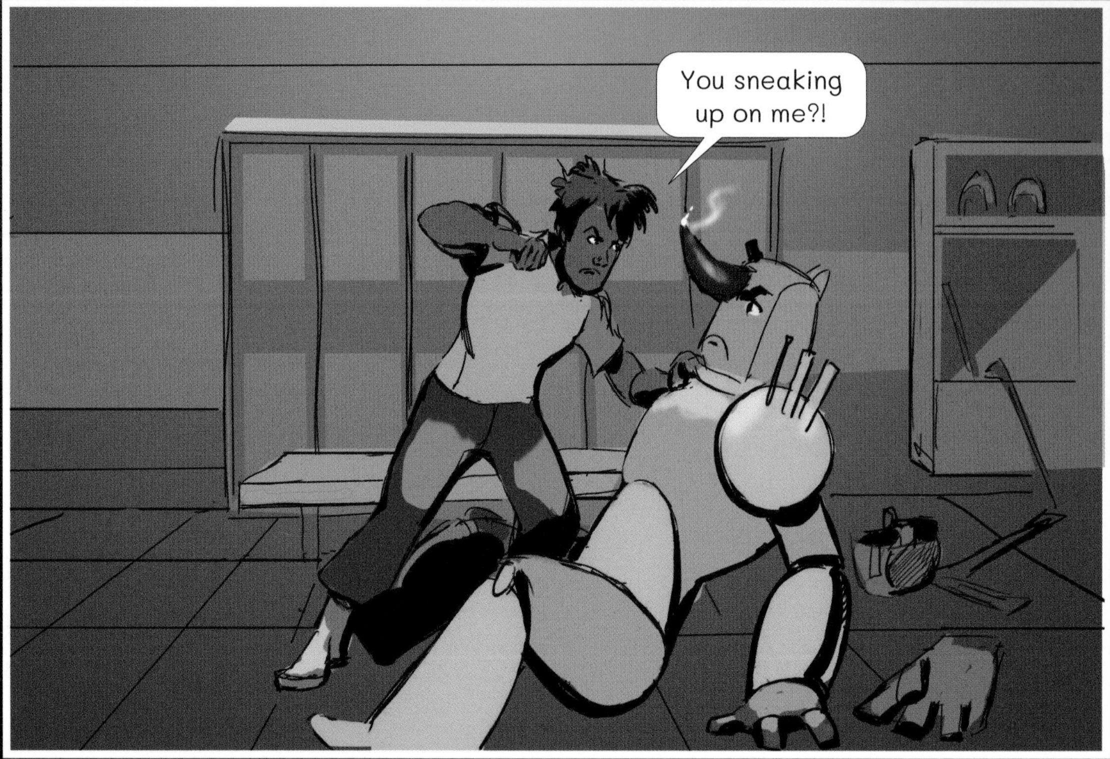
You sneaking up on me?!

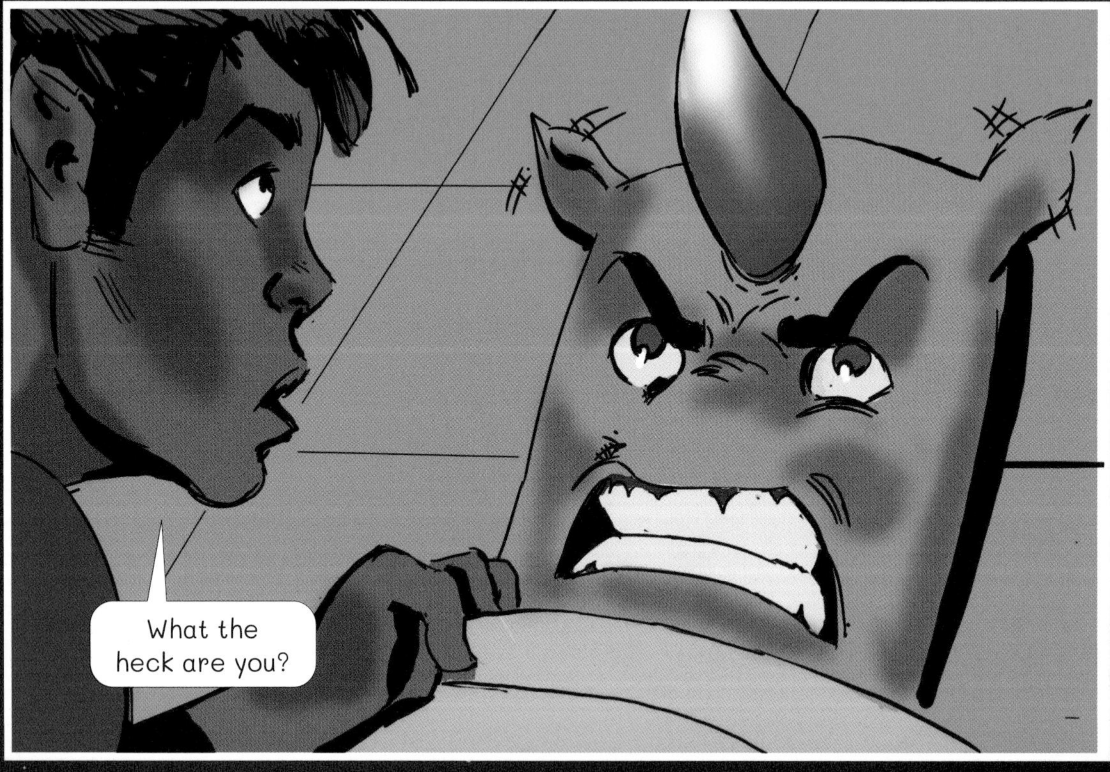
What the heck are you?

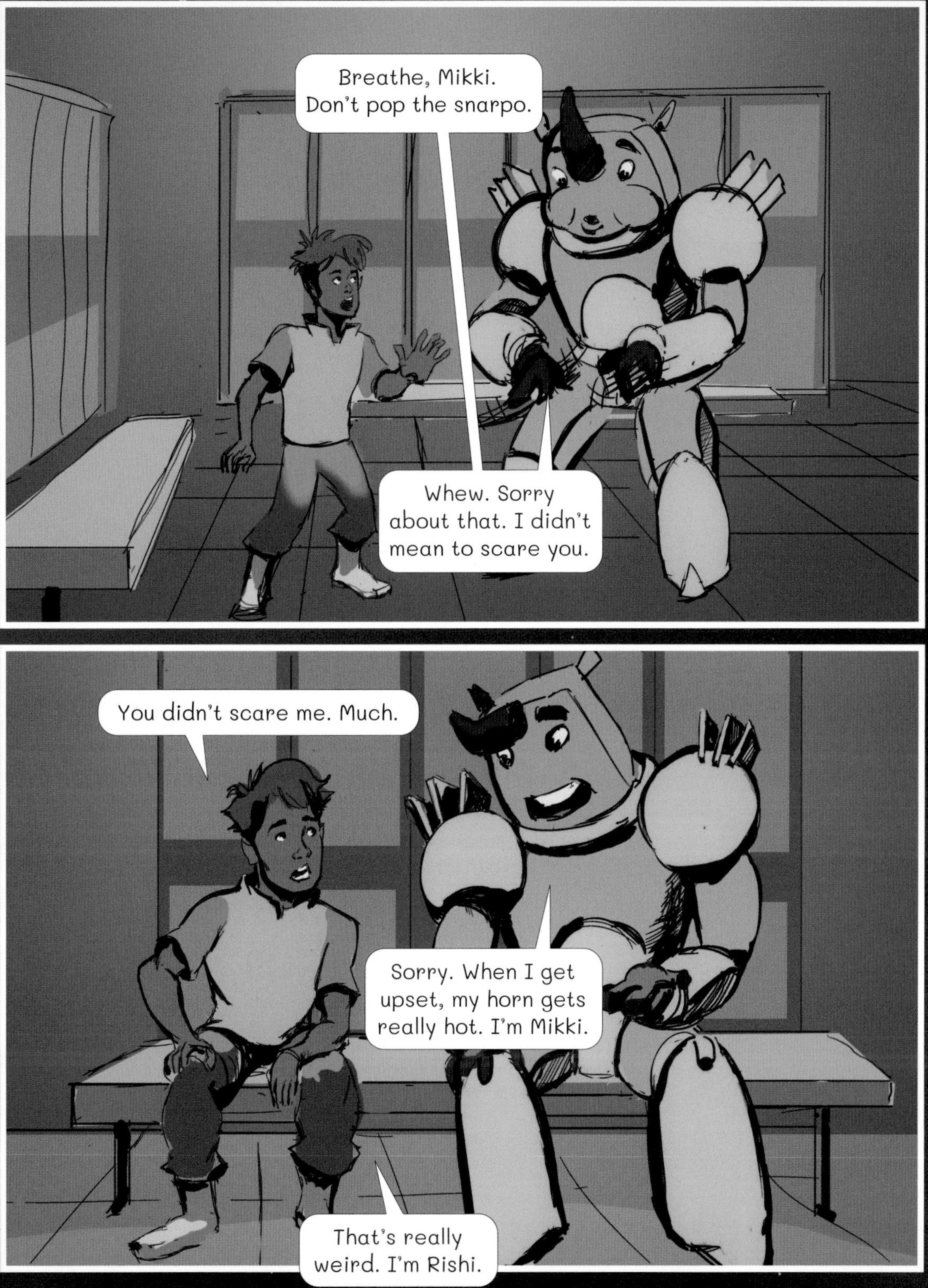
Breathe, Mikki. Don't pop the snarpo.
Whew. Sorry about that. I didn't mean to scare you.
You didn't scare me. Much.
Sorry. When I get upset, my horn gets really hot. I'm Mikki.
That's really weird. I'm Rishi.

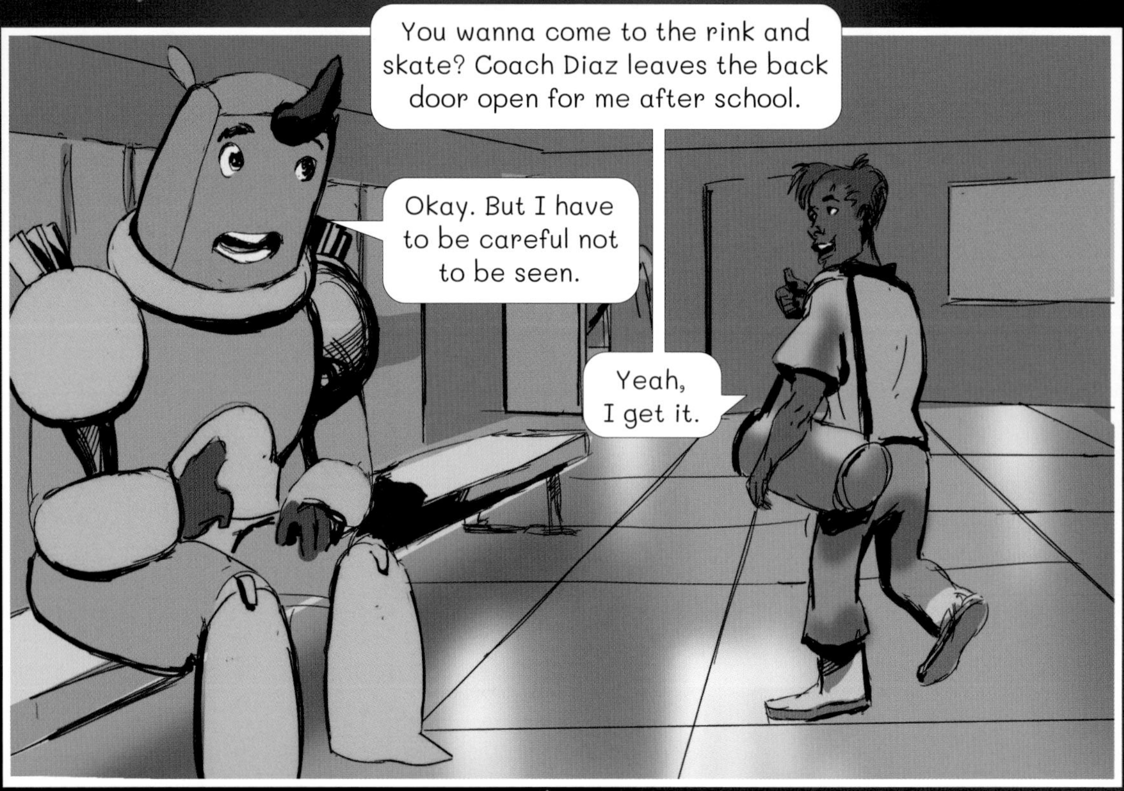
You wanna come to the rink and skate? Coach Diaz leaves the back door open for me after school.
Okay. But I have to be careful not to be seen.
Yeah, I get it.

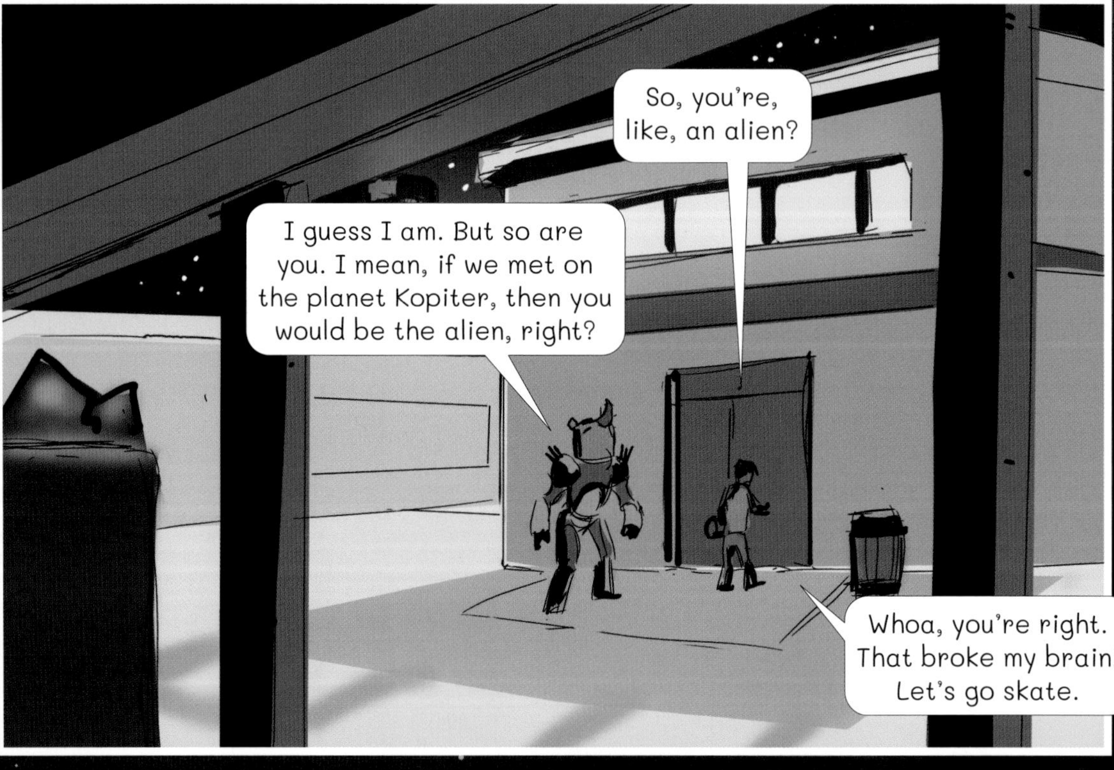
So, you're, like, an alien?
I guess I am. But so are you. I mean, if we met on the planet Kopiter, then you would be the alien, right?
Whoa, you're right. That broke my brain! Let's go skate.

THE GOAT

Wayne Gretzky is the greatest hockey player of all time. "The Great One" played 20 years in the NHL. He was the league's most valuable player 9 times. He earned each title during the first 10 years of his career.

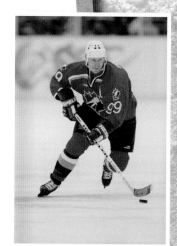

Gretzky led the league in scoring for 10 seasons. He is the only player to score 200 or more points in 1 season—and he did it 4 times! He is famous for his quote, "You miss 100 percent of the shots you don't take."

With Gretzky's help, the Edmonton Oilers won the Stanley Cup 4 times.

After his final year playing in 1999, the league **retired** his jersey number. Now, no other NHL player can ever wear the number 99.

retired: withdrew a jersey number from use

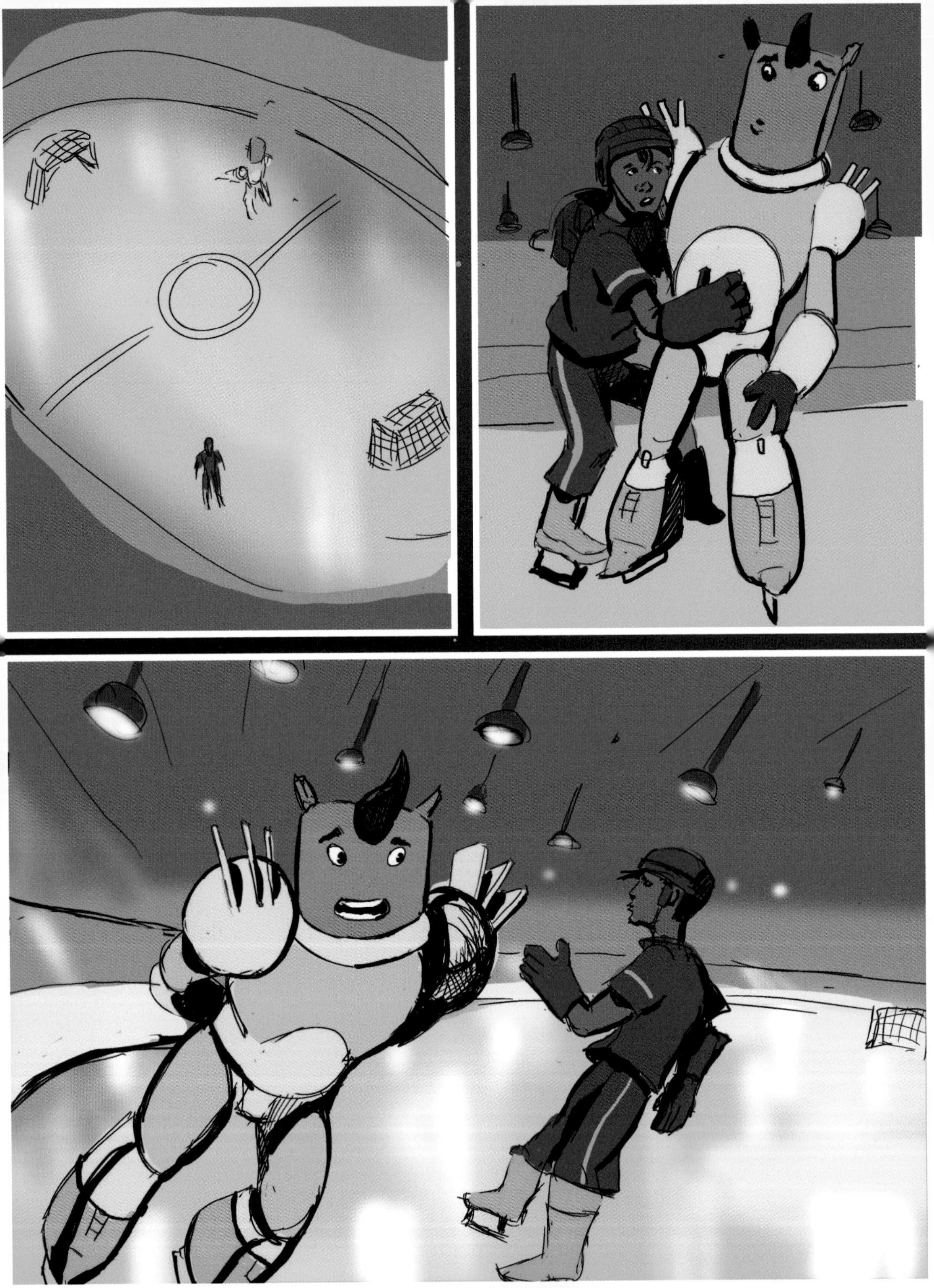

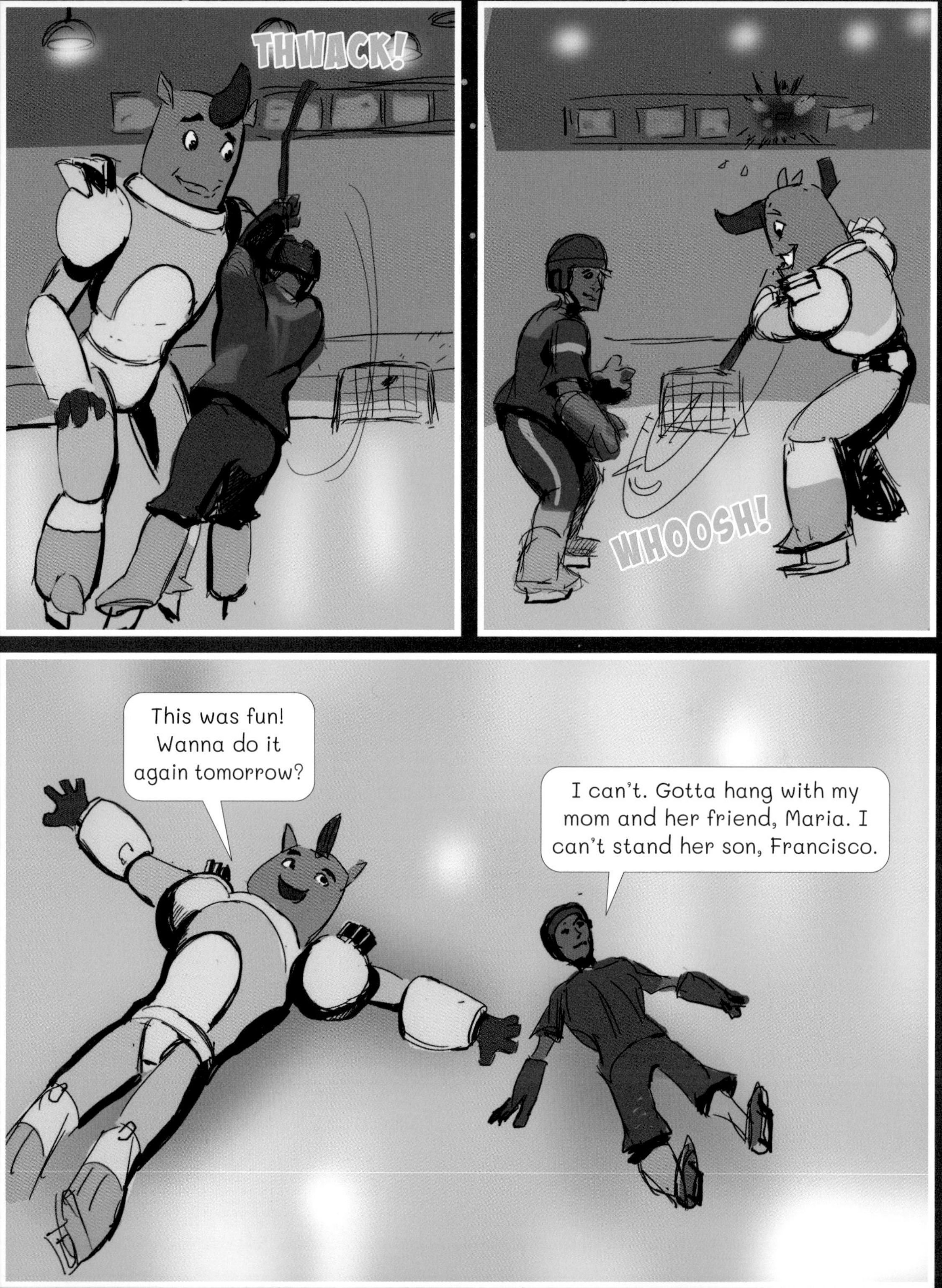
THWACK!
WHOOSH!
This was fun! Wanna do it again tomorrow?
I can't. Gotta hang with my mom and her friend, Maria. I can't stand her son, Francisco.

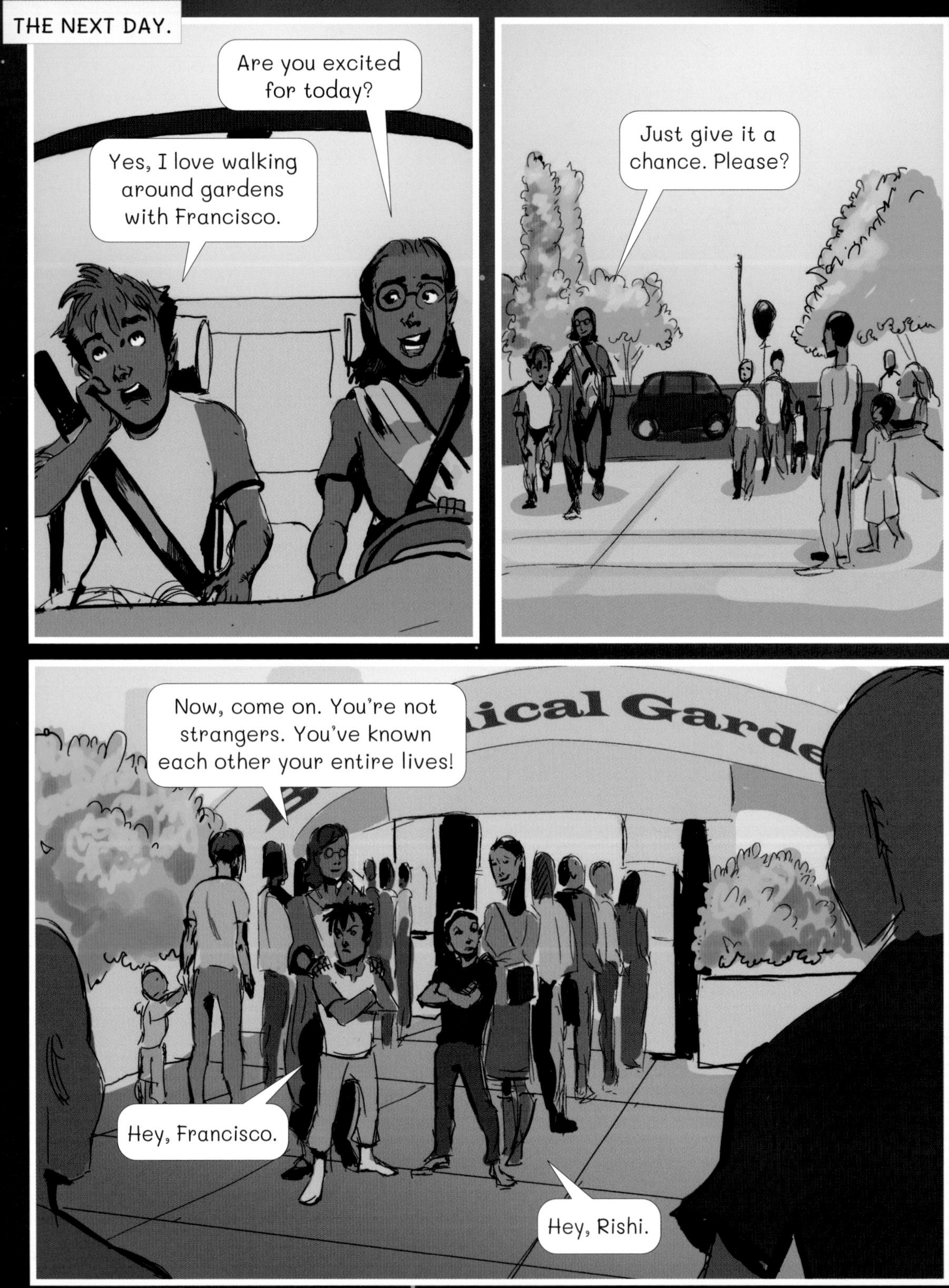
THE NEXT DAY.
Are you excited for today?
Yes, I love walking around gardens with Francisco.
Just give it a chance. Please?
Now, come on. You're not strangers. You've known each other your entire lives!
Hey, Francisco.
Hey, Rishi.

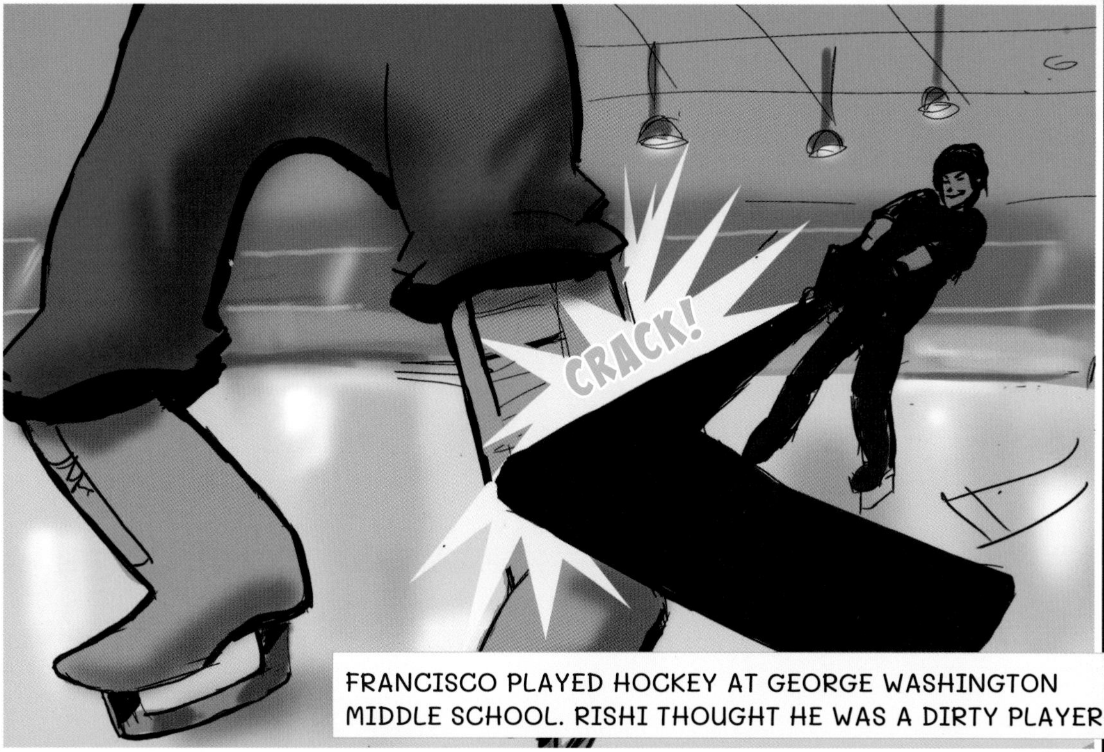
CRACK!
FRANCISCO PLAYED HOCKEY AT GEORGE WASHINGTON MIDDLE SCHOOL. RISHI THOUGHT HE WAS A DIRTY PLAYER.

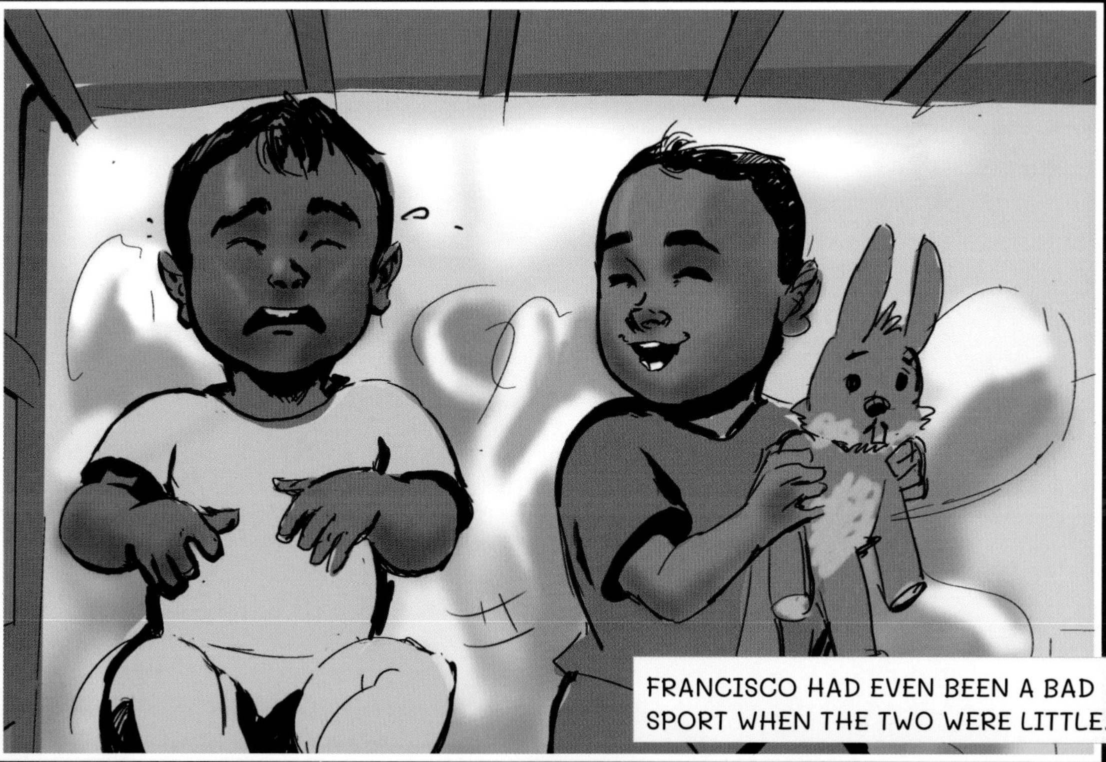
FRANCISCO HAD EVEN BEEN A BAD SPORT WHEN THE TWO WERE LITTLE.

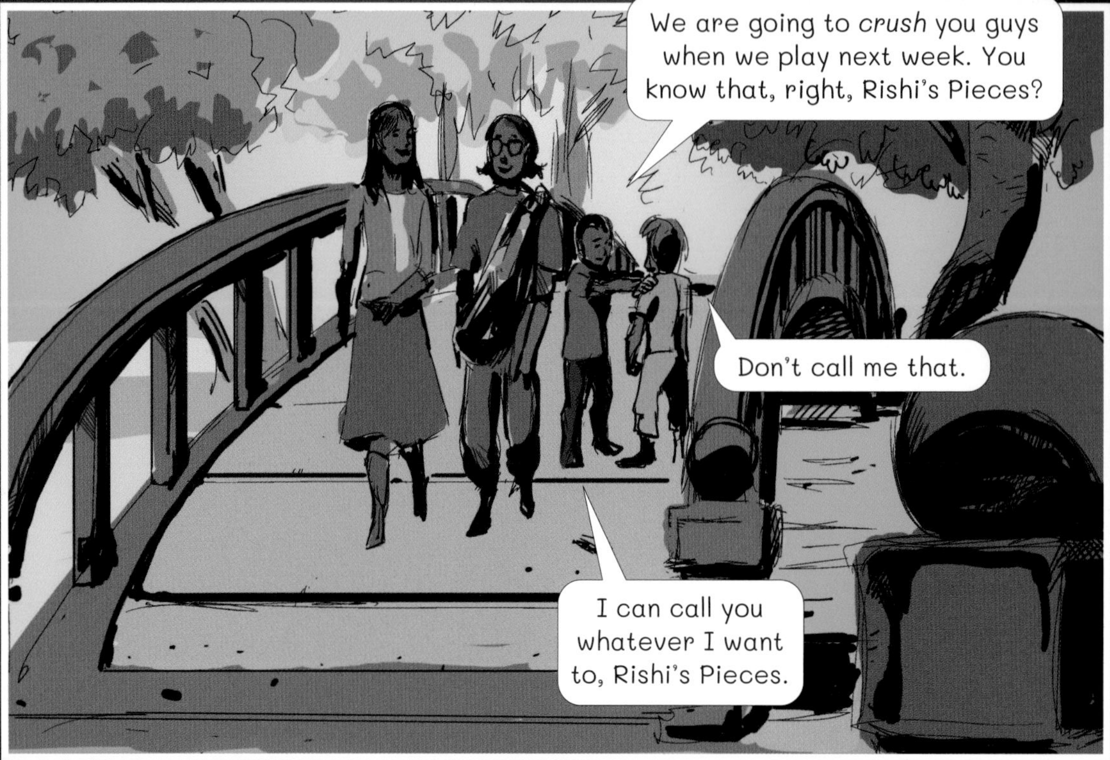
We are going to *crush* you guys when we play next week. You know that, right, Rishi's Pieces?
Don't call me that.
I can call you whatever I want to, Rishi's Pieces.

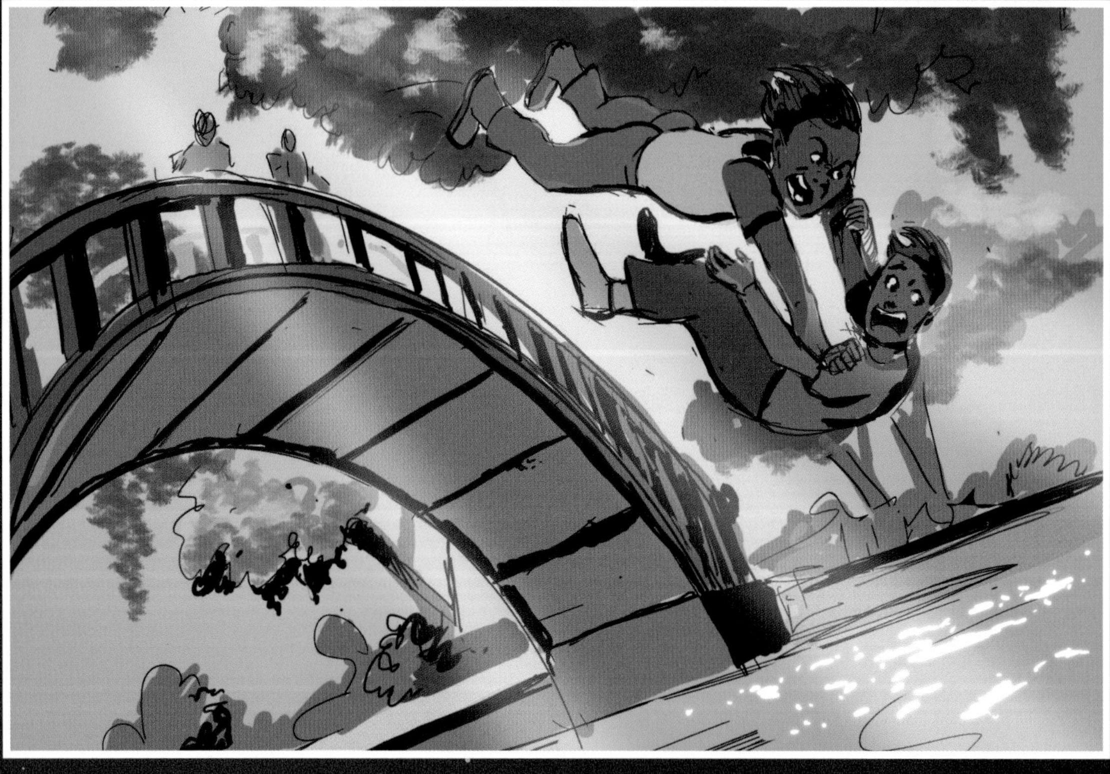

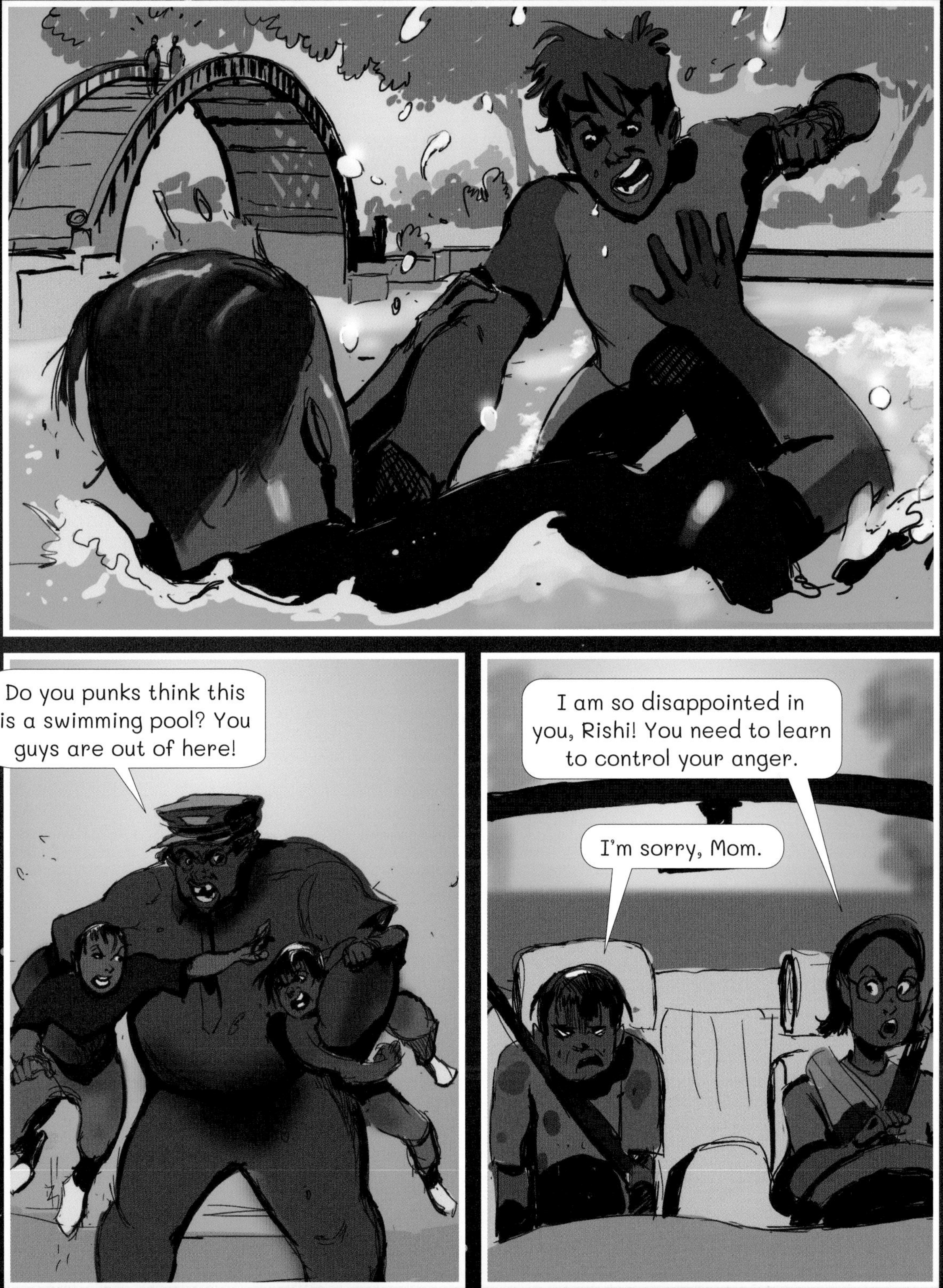
Do you punks think this is a swimming pool? You guys are out of here!
I am so disappointed in you, Rishi! You need to learn to control your anger.
I'm sorry, Mom.

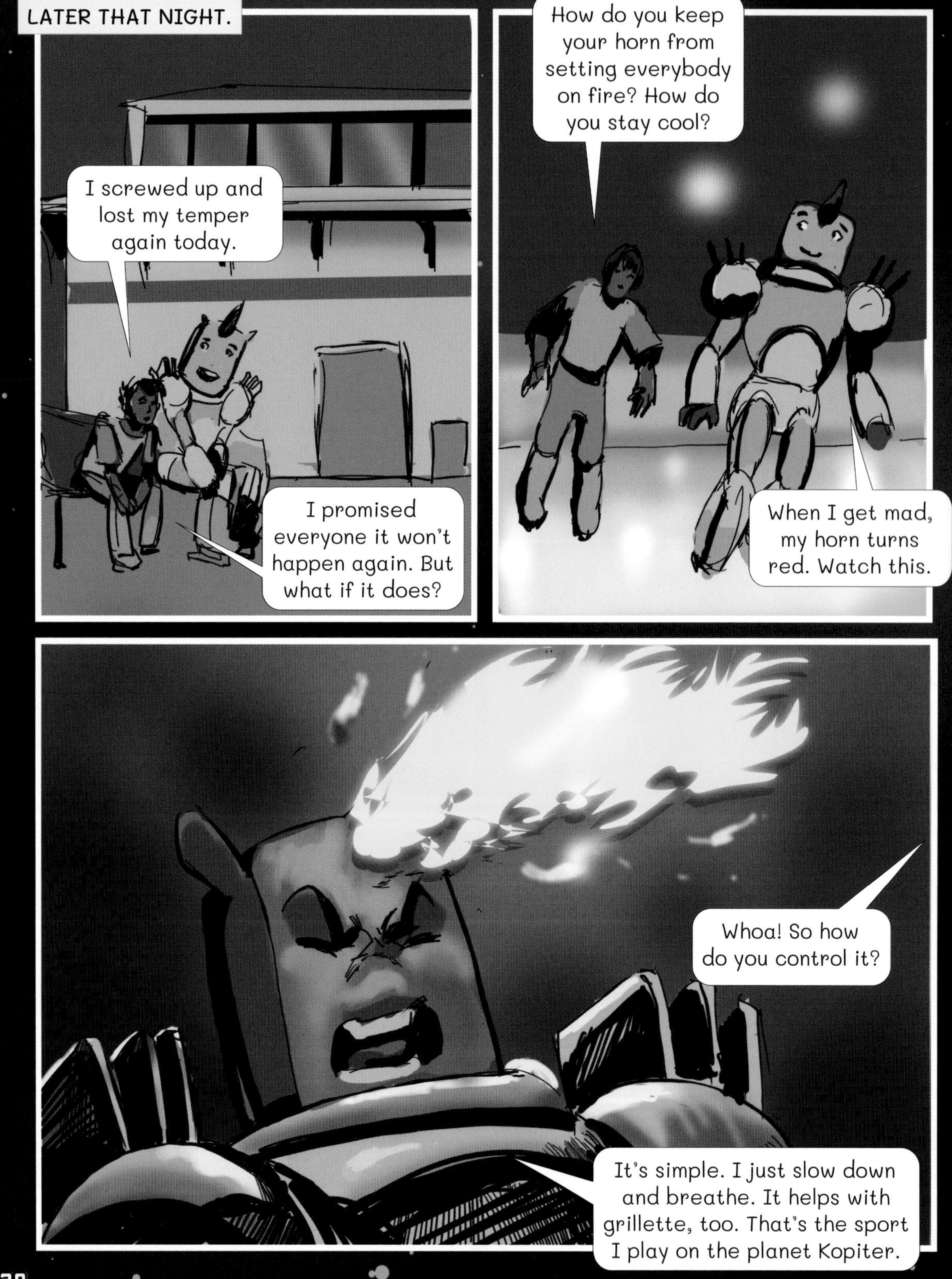
LATER THAT NIGHT.
I screwed up and lost my temper again today.
I promised everyone it won't happen again. But what if it does?
How do you keep your horn from setting everybody on fire? How do you stay cool?
When I get mad, my horn turns red. Watch this.
Whoa! So how do you control it?
It's simple. I just slow down and breathe. It helps with grillette, too. That's the sport I play on the planet Kopiter.

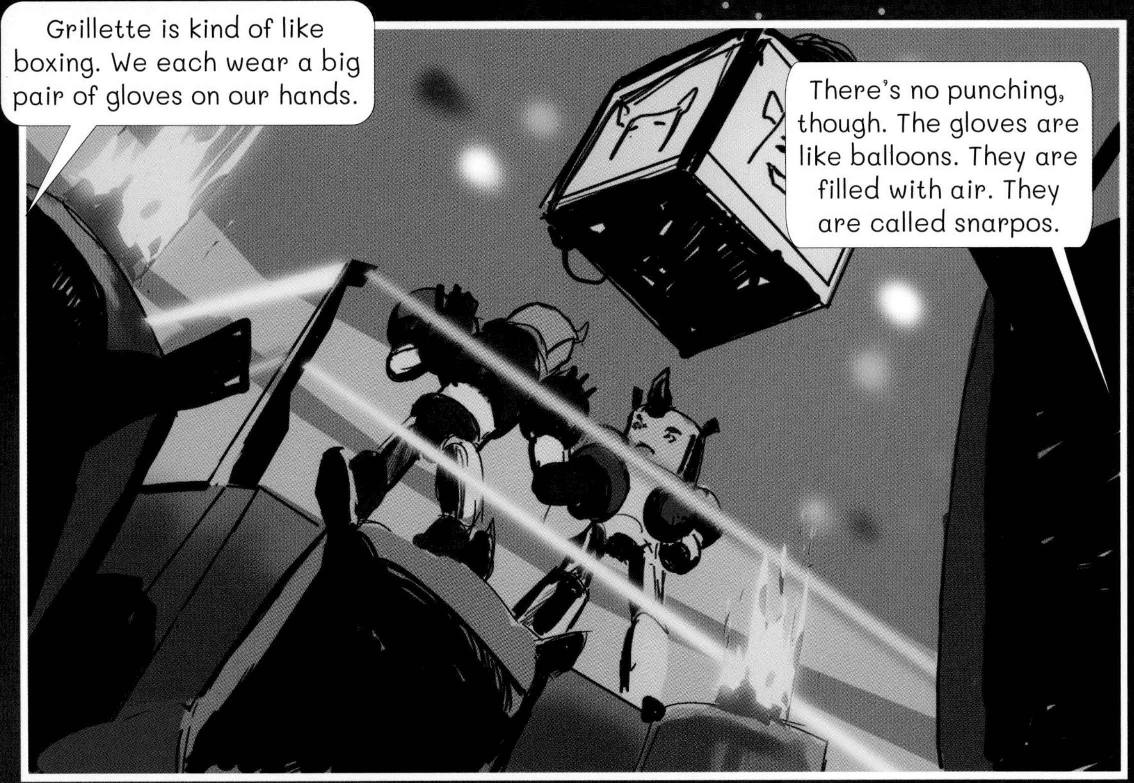
Grillette is kind of like boxing. We each wear a big pair of gloves on our hands.
There's no punching, though. The gloves are like balloons. They are filled with air. They are called snarpos.

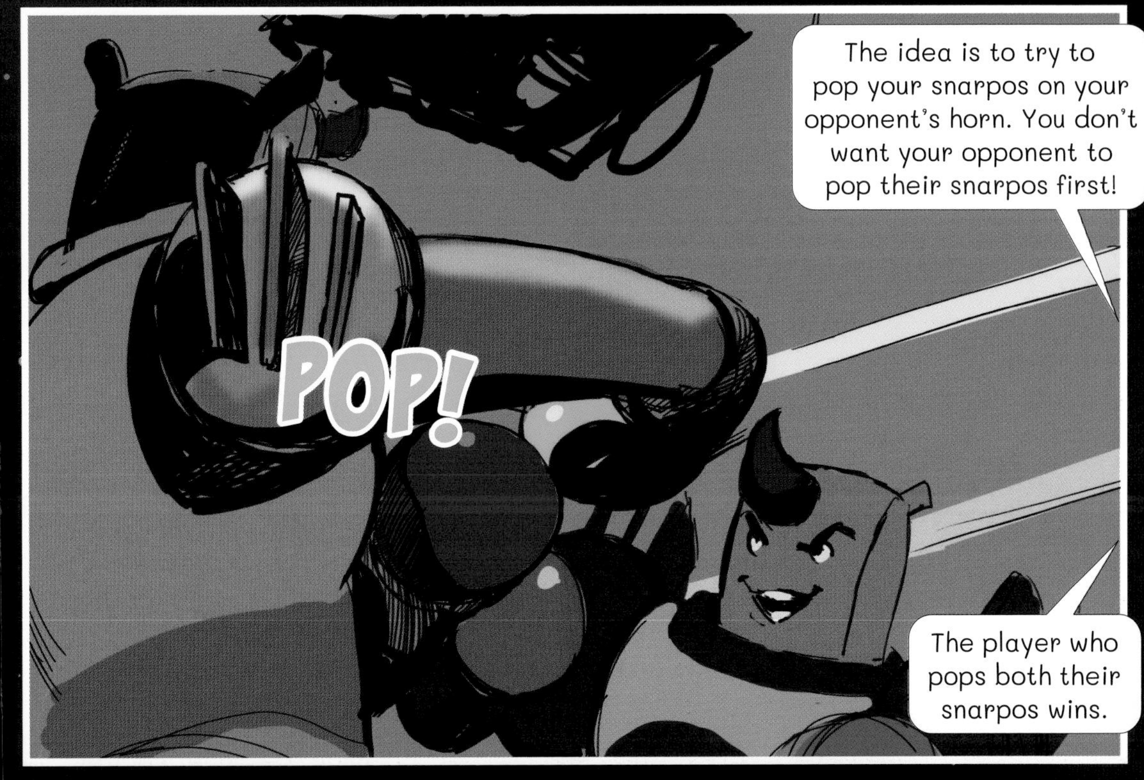
The idea is to try to pop your snarpos on your opponent's horn. You don't want your opponent to pop their snarpos first!
POP!
The player who pops both their snarpos wins.

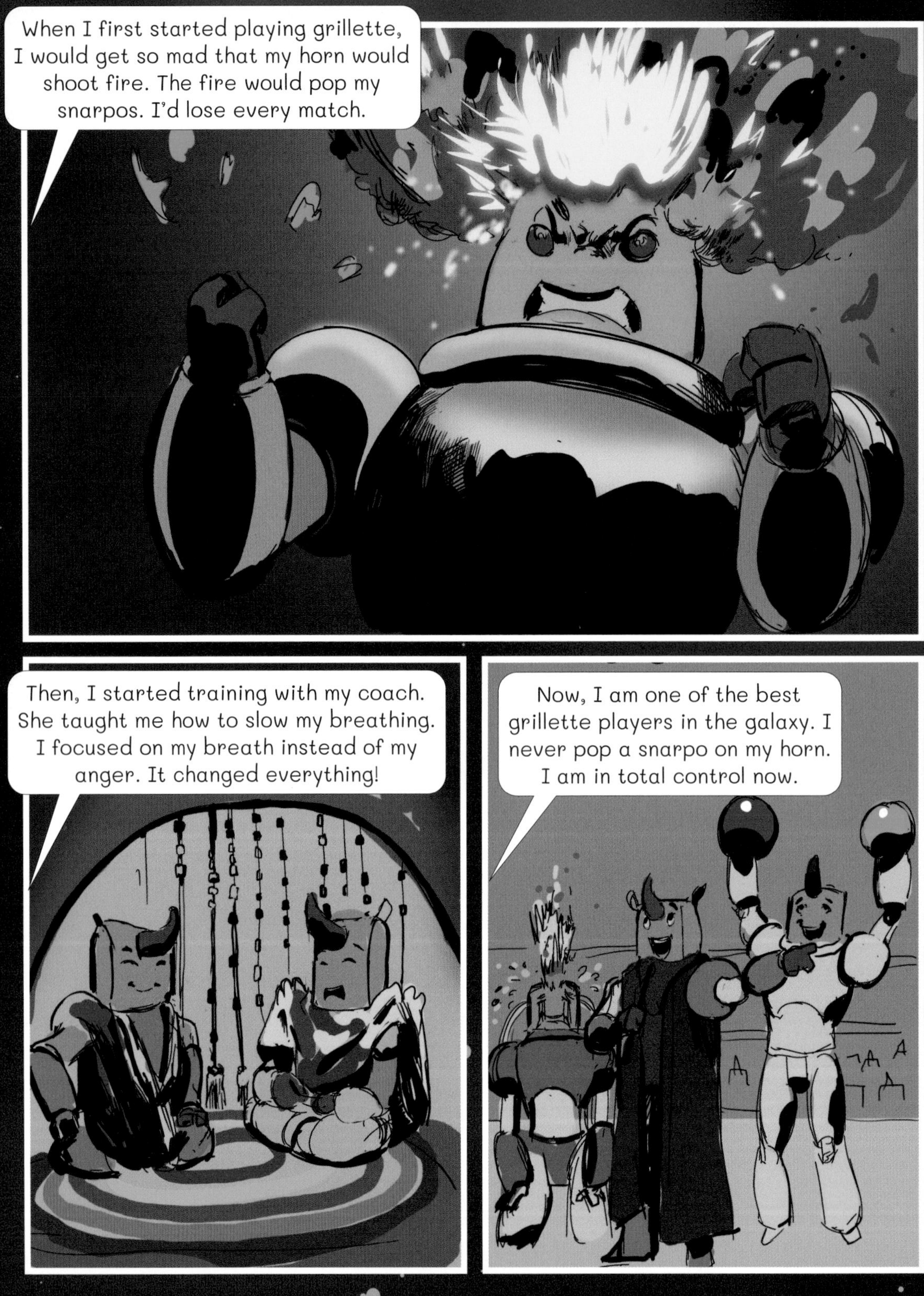
When I first started playing grillette, I would get so mad that my horn would shoot fire. The fire would pop my snarpos. I'd lose every match.
Then, I started training with my coach. She taught me how to slow my breathing. I focused on my breath instead of my anger. It changed everything!
Now, I am one of the best grillette players in the galaxy. I never pop a snarpo on my horn. I am in total control now.

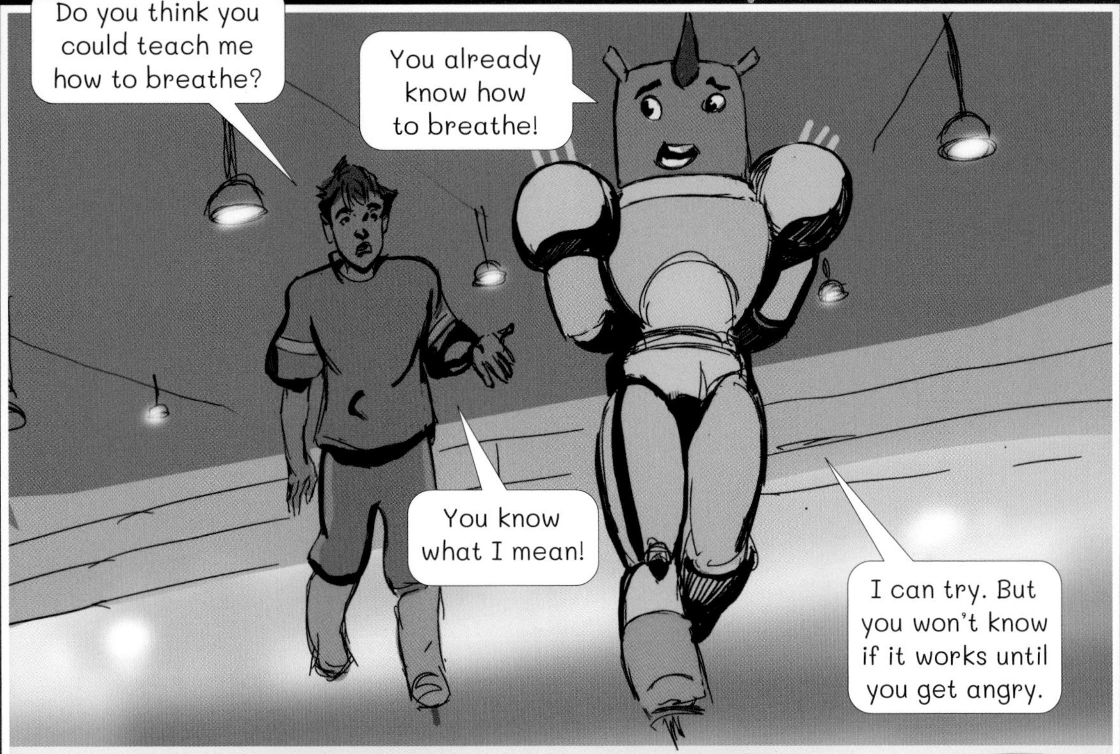
Do you think you could teach me how to breathe?
You already know how to breathe!
You know what I mean!
I can try. But you won't know if it works until you get angry.

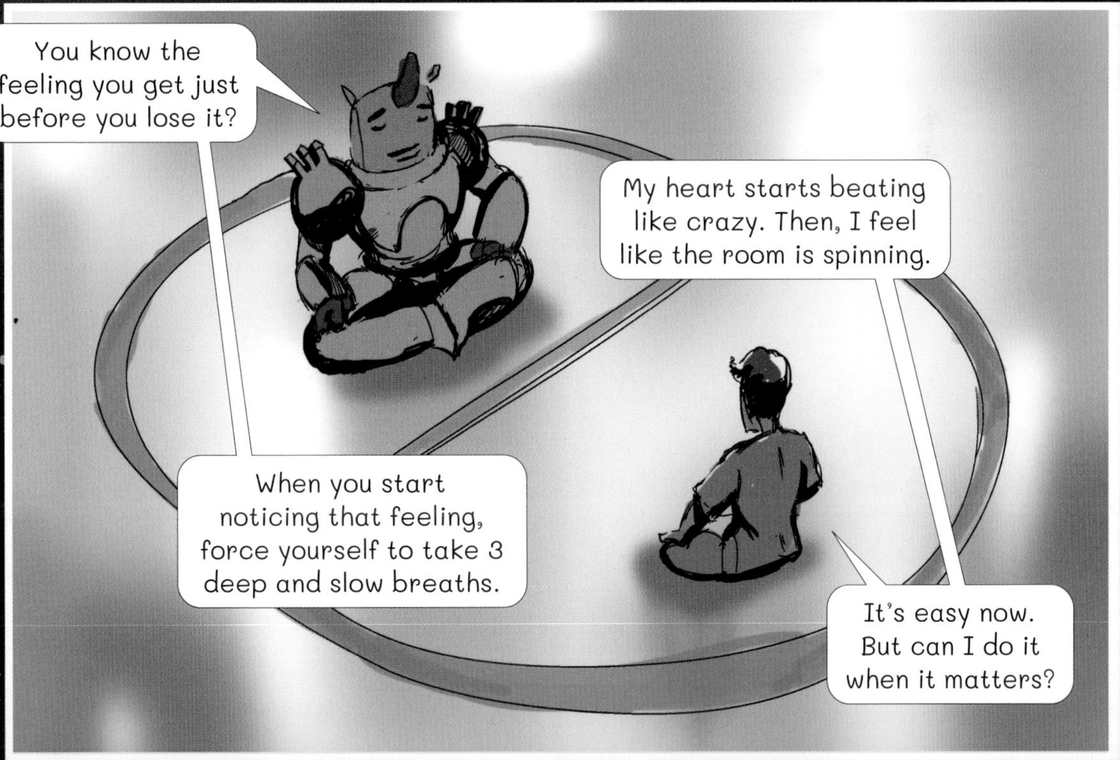
You know the feeling you get just before you lose it?
My heart starts beating like crazy. Then, I feel like the room is spinning.
When you start noticing that feeling, force yourself to take 3 deep and slow breaths.
It's easy now. But can I do it when it matters?

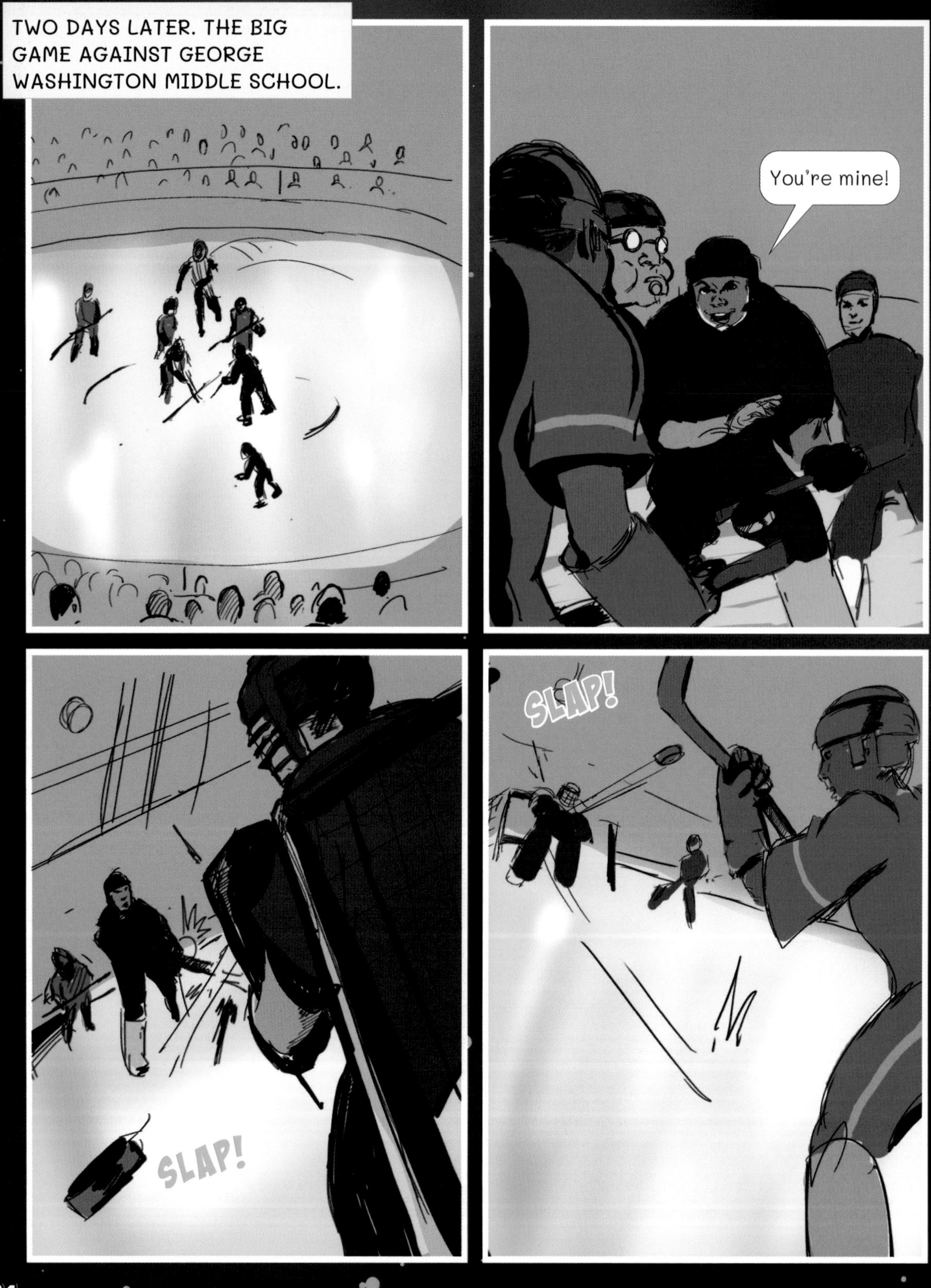
TWO DAYS LATER. THE BIG GAME AGAINST GEORGE WASHINGTON MIDDLE SCHOOL.
You're mine!
SLAP!
SLAP!

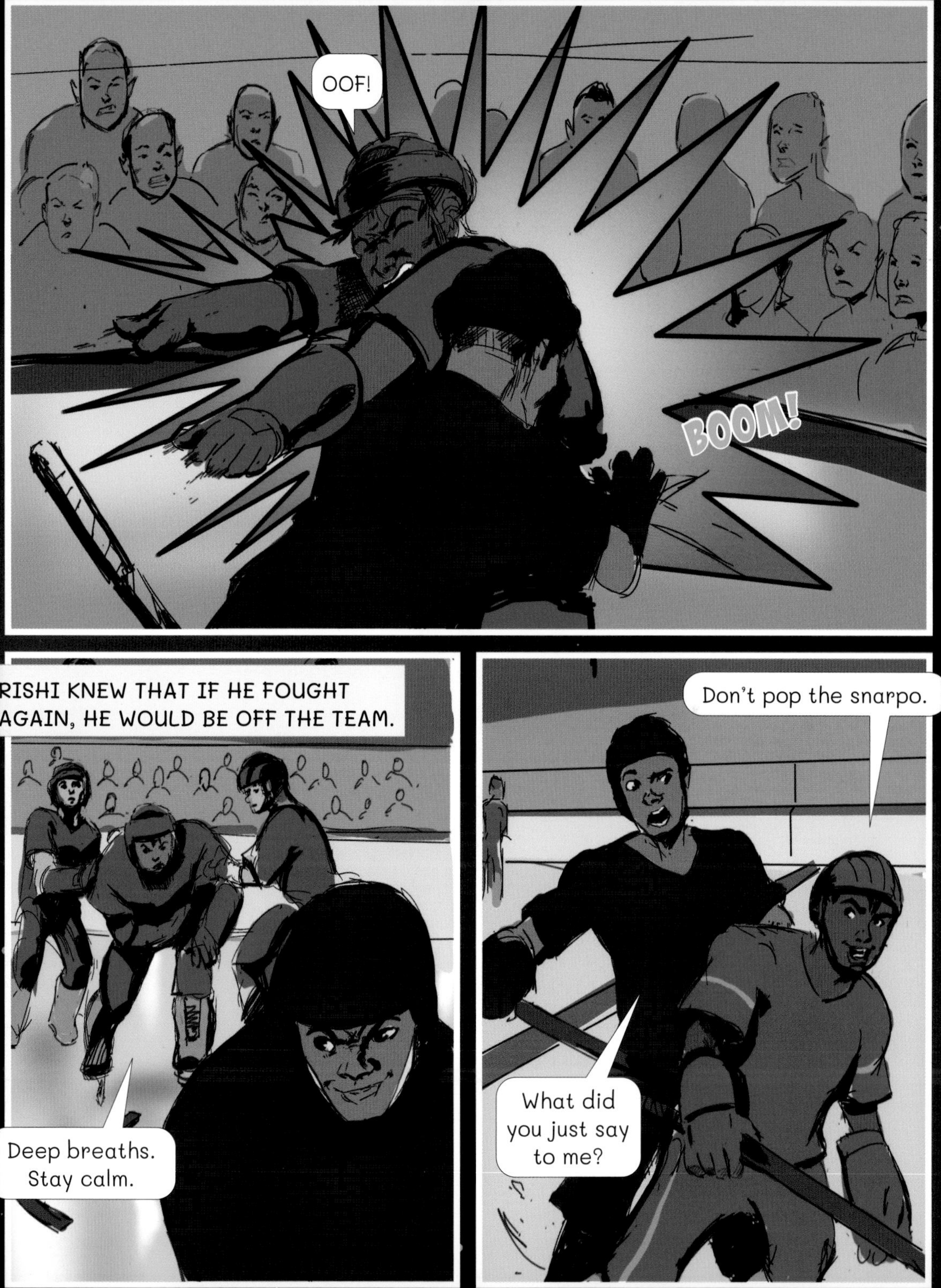
OOF!
BOOM!
RISHI KNEW THAT IF HE FOUGHT AGAIN, HE WOULD BE OFF THE TEAM.
Deep breaths. Stay calm.
Don't pop the snarpo.
What did you just say to me?

1—0, JACKIE ROBINSON MIDDLE SCHOOL WINS!

BZZT!

THUMP!

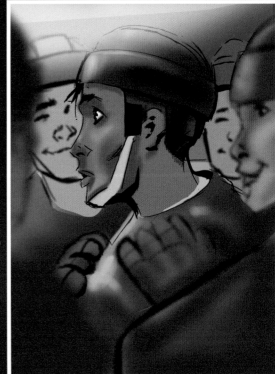

MINDFULNESS

It's easy to get caught up in the moment. Sometimes, we act before we are able to think things through.

Being mindful means stopping to think about what you are feeling. It can be hard to do this. Feeling angry, sad, or frustrated is normal. Slowing down to recognize these feelings before reacting is key. You are in control. Your actions have a huge impact on those around you.

Keeping your cool during a game can be a challenge. Reacting with anger or frustration will land you in the penalty box. The best players still feel their feelings, but they don't let those feelings control their actions.

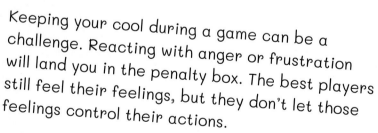

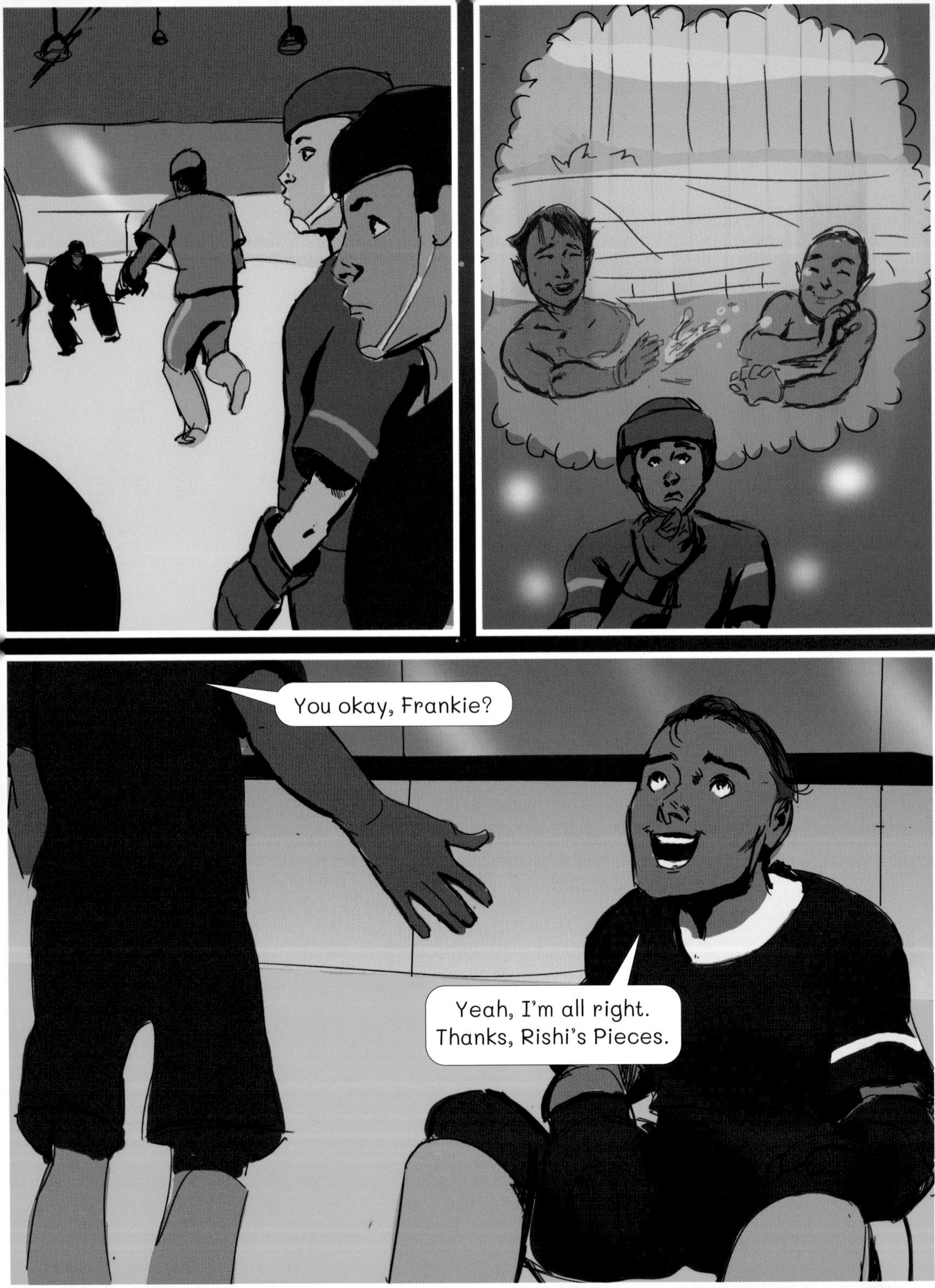
You okay, Frankie?
Yeah, I'm all right.
Thanks, Rishi's Pieces.

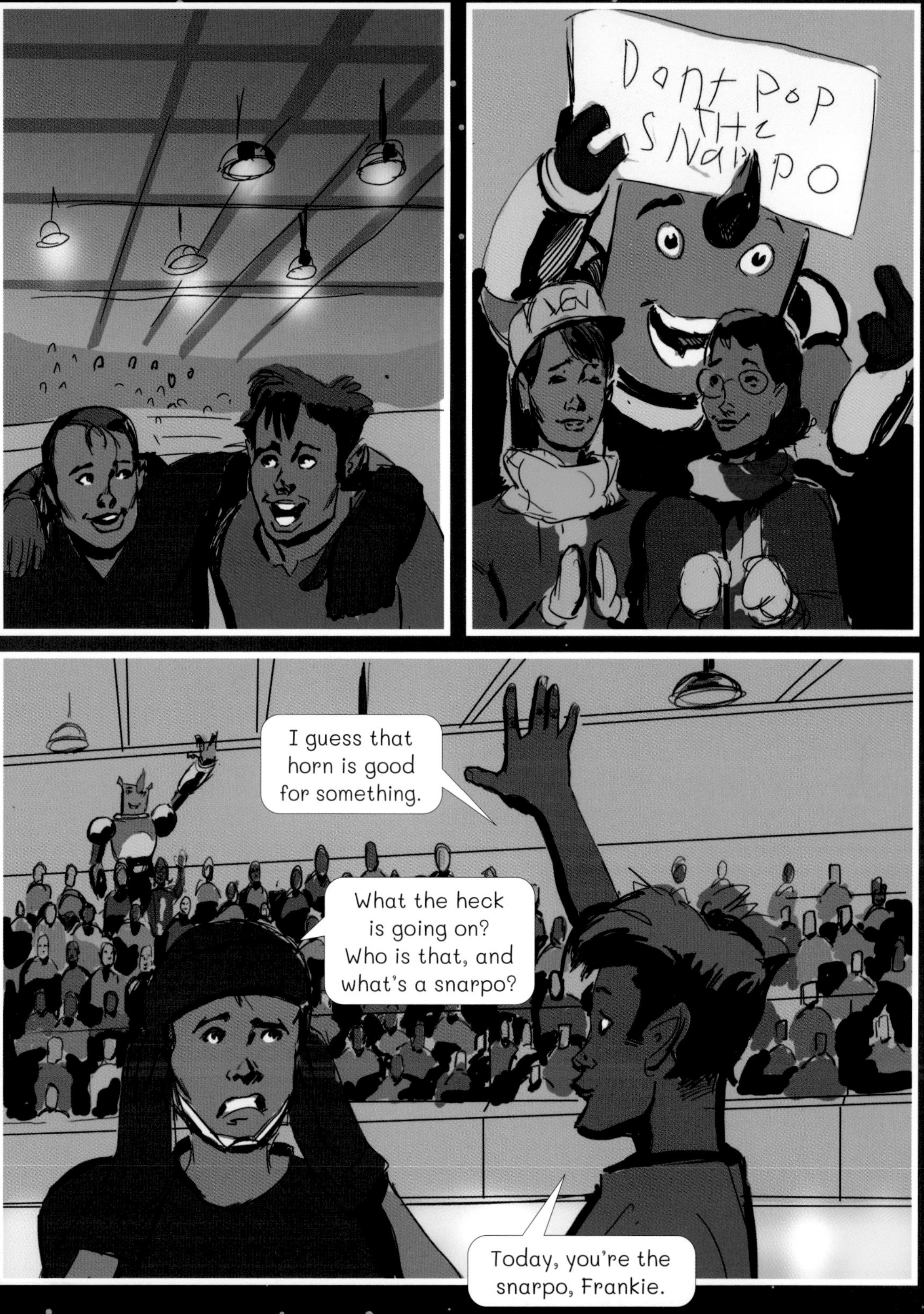
Dont Pop the SNarpo
I guess that horn is good for something.
What the heck is going on? Who is that, and what's a snarpo?
Today, you're the snarpo, Frankie.

FIND YOUR HAPPY PLACE

Inside all of us is a happy place. Find this place and go there to feel calm and peaceful.

What You Need
* colored pencils
* paper

Steps to Take

1. Write the words *My Happy Place* on a sheet of paper. Draw a picture of yourself at the bottom. Draw 5 large clouds around you.

2. Write a sentence in each cloud:
   I can smell:
   I can hear:
   I can see:
   I can taste:
   I can touch:

3. In each cloud, write smells, sounds, sights, tastes, and touches that make you feel happy. When you feel stressed, think back to the things you wrote.

LEARN MORE

BOOKS

Doeden, Matt. *Hockey's Wickedest Goals!* North Mankato, MN: Capstone Press, 2021.

Herman, Gail. *What Is the Stanley Cup?* New York, NY: Penguin Workshop, 2019.

WEBSITES

Gretzky's Story
https://www.gretzky.com/bio.php

KidsKonnect: Hockey
https://kidskonnect.com/sports/hockey

ALIEN CHARACTERS

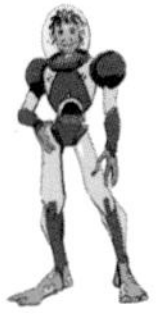

DARNEX

DARNEX IS A HETHITE FROM THE PLANET HETHA. ON HIS HOME PLANET, HE PLAYS THE SPORT WAVE RIDER. HIS BODY MAKES A STICKY GOO THAT SMELLS LIKE PINEAPPLE.

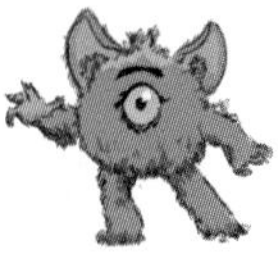

ZANG

ZANG IS AN ALIEN FROM PLANET SMONGTHURP. HE IS A PRO AT THE SPORT FLONGLOG, AND A PRO AT SIGN LANGUAGE.

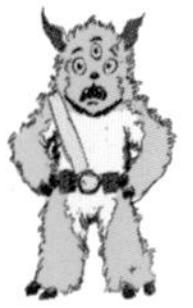

SPLART

SPLART IS AN ALIEN FROM THE PLANET TRASPEN. HE LOVES EATING BACON AND BASEBALLS. HE PLAYS SWAZBUL. IMAGINING FLOWERS AND SANDWICHES HELPS HIM RELAX.

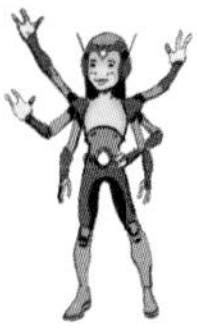

FORBATH

FORBATH IS AN ALIEN FROM THE PLANET EXBERG. SHE PLAYS THE SPORT THREE-SKIFF, WHICH MAKES HER A MASTER MULTITASKER.

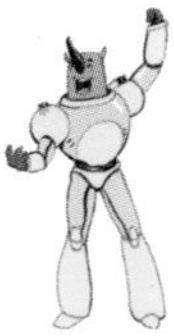

MIKKI

MIKKI IS AN ALIEN FROM PLANET KOPITER. HIS SPORT IS GRILLETTE. HE HAS WORKED HARD TO KEEP HIS COOL UNDER PRESSURE.

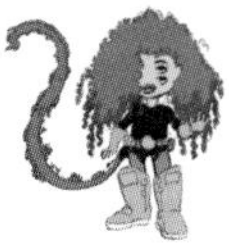

BOLI

BOLI IS AN ALIEN FROM THE PLANET OOH. SHE PLAYS THE TEAM SPORT ZINGER. SHE IS A GREAT TEAMMATE AND FRIEND TO EVERYONE.

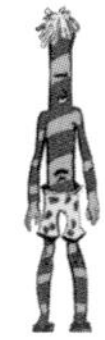

GAMEE GLAP

GAMEE IS AN ALIEN FROM THE PLANET MOOBSTRUM. HE IS A FLARFELL DIVE STAR. HE KNOWS HOW TO HANDLE BULLIES.

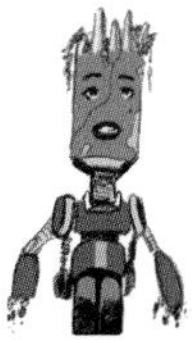

DREEPY

DREEPY IS AN INTERGALACTIC SPORTS STAR, AND SHE KNOWS IT. HER PLANET VALUES HONESTY OVER EVERYTHING. WHO WANTS TO GET SQUASHED BY A TRUTHY BOOT?

GLOSSARY

checked (CHEKD) when one player crashes into the player controlling the puck

galaxy (GAL-uk-see) a system of stars and their solar systems

intergalactic (in-tuhr-guh-LAK-tik) between galaxies in space

meteor shower (MEE-tee-uhr SHOW-uhr) a group of space rocks that fall as they enter Earth's atmosphere

penalty (PEN-uhl-tee) a punishment for breaking the rules; in hockey, a player is forced to sit in the penalty box for 2 to 4 minutes. Their teammates must play without them.

penalty box (PEN-uhl-tee BOX) an area where a player serves their penalty time

power play (POW-uhr PLAY) a period of time during a hockey game where at least one opposing player is in the penalty box

retired (ruh-TY-uhrd) withdrew a jersey number from use

INDEX